BOY SCOUTS OF AMERICA
MERIT BADGE SERIES

# LAW

*"Enhancing our youths' competitive edge through merit badges"*

BOY SCOUTS OF AMERICA®

# Requirements

1. Define "law." Tell some of its sources. Describe functions it serves.

2. Discuss two of the following:

    a. Justinian's Code, the Code of Hammurabi, and the Magna Carta

    b. The development of the jury system

    c. Two famous trials in history

3. Tell what civil law is; tell what criminal law is. Tell the main differences between them. Give examples of each.

4. Ask five people (not more than one from your immediate family) about the role of law enforcement officers in our society. Discuss their answers with them. Go to a law enforcement officer in your neighborhood and ask about his or her responsibilities and duties. Report your findings.

5. Tell about several laws that were passed to protect the consumer and the seller. Tell about several organizations that provide help to consumers and sellers.

6. Do one of the following:

    a. Attend a session of a civil or criminal court. Write 250 words or more on what you saw.

    b. Plan and conduct a mock trial with your troop or school class. After the trial is over, discuss it with the group.

7. Arrange a visit with a lawyer who works for a business, bank, title company, or government agency. Find out his or her duties and responsibilities. Report what you have learned.

8. Explain the requirements for becoming a lawyer in your state. Describe how judges are selected in your state.

9. Make a list of 15 jobs that deal with some aspects of law or legal processes. Tell which you prefer. Why?

10. Tell where people can go to obtain the help of a lawyer if they are unable to pay for one. Tell what you can do if you can afford a lawyer but do not know of any in your area.

11. Discuss with your counselor the importance in our society of TWO of the following areas of the law:

    a. Environmental law
    b. Computers and the internet
    c. Copyright and the internet
    d. Immigration
    e. Patents
    f. Biotechnology
    g. Privacy law
    h. International law

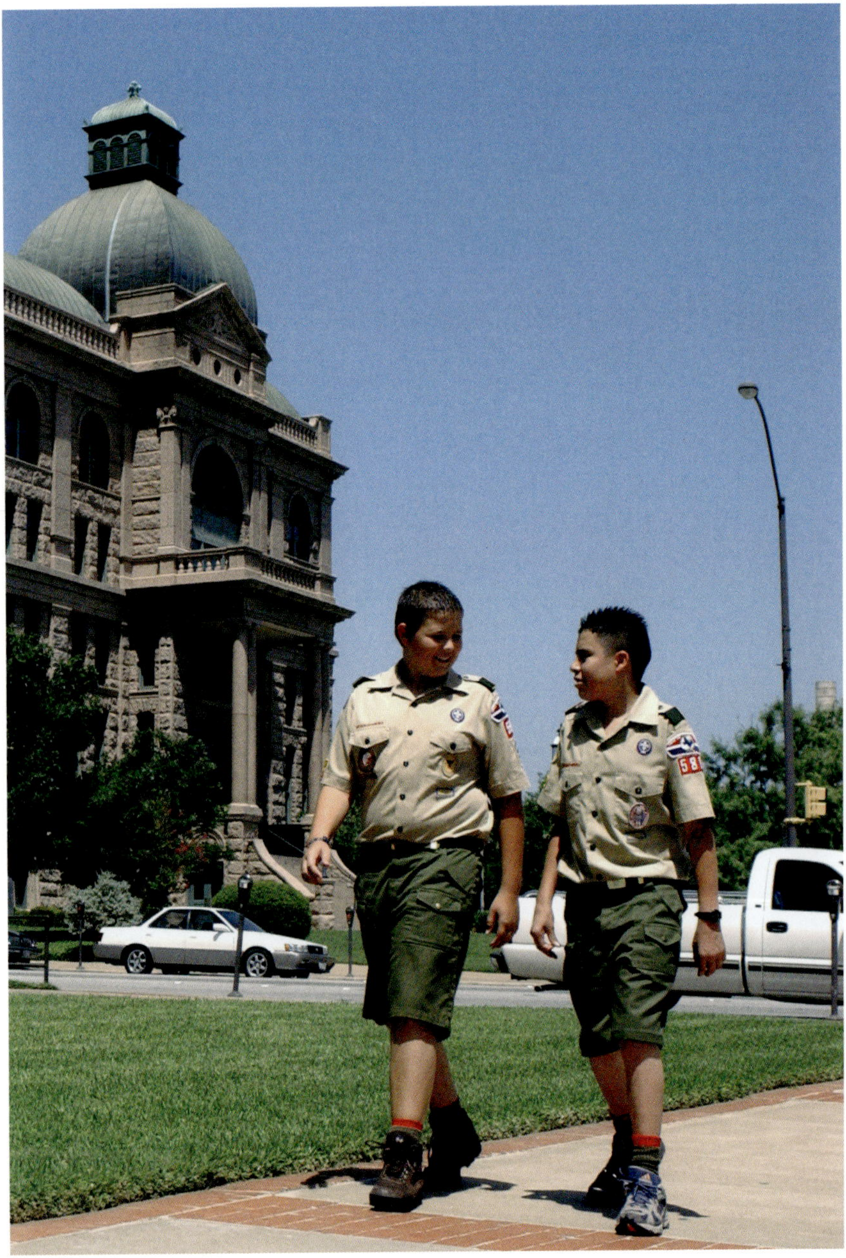

# Contents

What Is Law? . . . . . . . . . . . . . . . . . . . . . . . . . . . . . . . . 7

Great Beginnings: Where Law Comes From . . . . . . . . . . . . . 15

Civil and Criminal Law . . . . . . . . . . . . . . . . . . . . . . . . . . 27

Law Enforcement: More Than a Gun and a Badge . . . . . . . . 35

Organizations That Help Protect Consumers and Sellers . . . . 49

The Law in Action. . . . . . . . . . . . . . . . . . . . . . . . . . . . . 51

Planning a Mock Trial . . . . . . . . . . . . . . . . . . . . . . . . . . 59

Emerging Law. . . . . . . . . . . . . . . . . . . . . . . . . . . . . . . 67

Careers in the Legal Profession . . . . . . . . . . . . . . . . . . . . 74

Resources About Law . . . . . . . . . . . . . . . . . . . . . . . . . . 78

588
The Dallas Morning News
tax appraisal
skyrocket
Rogers stays

# What Is Law?

Camporees are great! There's a lot to do: swimming, good fishing, adventure trails, and hiking expeditions. There's the skill-o-rama, where you can see how troops do things like specialty cooking and arts and crafts. And huge arena shows draw audiences in the tens of thousands.

This is the story of some Scouts who met at a camporee and how a bull session there got them interested in law. One of them, named Jeff, a First Class Scout, went on to earn his Law merit badge. How did he do it? Read on to find out.

Jeff is a lot like you. He likes sports. He's got a good record in Scouting. He's pretty good in school—not great maybe, but not bad. He likes to hike and go camping.

One afternoon at the camporee, Jeff was walking around with Raul, an Eagle Scout from another troop. They found a newspaper on a bench, so they sat down to check the sports page. Jeff finished first and glanced at the front page.

"Hey, Raul," Jeff said, "there's a sports story on the front page, too. This headline says, 'Stephens Wins Court Battle.' It must be a story about a tennis match!" He laughed, enjoying his joke.

Raul said, "Ha, ha," and continued reading the sports page.

Jeff read the front-page story, which was about a long trial in a Texas court. "This is a real interesting case. This guy Stephens sued the city for polluting a river with sewage—and won! It's hard to believe one guy could beat city hall."

Raul looked up from the sports pages. "Well," he said, "I guess there are lots of laws that we don't know anything about. And I guess you can get justice," he said uncertainly.

Just then Marcus, a Scout whom Jeff and Raul had met earlier, walked up. "Hey, what are you guys doing?"

Jeff laughed. "We started out reading the sports page. But all of a sudden we are wondering about the law and courts and stuff like that."

# What Is Law?

"Yeah?" Marcus said. "My Scoutmaster, Ms. Roth, is a lawyer. If you guys aren't doing anything, let's go down to the waterfront and talk to her. She's fishing down there, I think."

The three Scouts found Ms. Roth on the dock with her line in the water and three beautiful trout on a string. "Hi, guys," Ms. Roth said. "Want to try your luck?"

Marcus said: "Not right now, Ms. Roth. This is Jeff and Raul. We wanted to talk to you about law. Jeff and Raul were reading an article in the paper about a trial in Texas. One thing led to another . . . and here we are with some questions."

"Sure. Sit down, guys," Ms. Roth said. She reeled in her line as they plopped down next to her. Jeff began explaining that the story about the Texas trial had raised questions in his mind. "Where does law come from? What is it really?" Jeff asked. Marcus wanted to know what's special about lawyers and how a young person becomes one. Raul wanted to know how law affects his own life.

> Law is a system of ideas and actions, a way to help society keep order and stay together.

## Law Is Different Things to Different People

"Whoa, guys!" said Ms. Roth. "One question at a time. Let's start with the first one: What is law? That may sound like an easy question, but there are many ways to define law. Every judge, every lawyer, every police officer—maybe every American—has different ideas of what it is. Law serves many purposes and means different things to different people."

Marcus broke in. "To me, laws are rules. They say what you can do and what you can't do, like going through a red light or stealing. . . ."

"Or hurting someone on purpose," Raul added.

"But laws often help people, too," Ms. Roth said. "Law is much more than just a set of rules."

Some years ago, Ms. Roth recalled, President Lyndon B. Johnson spoke to Scouts at a national Scout jamboree. He told them that the American idea of freedom allows all citizens to speak their view, worship as they want to, and be safe from actions the government has no right to take. "President Johnson also said that the equality of the poorest people and the richest, the rights to enjoy liberty and go as far as your abilities will take you, are all upheld and backed by the U.S. legal system."

Raul said: "I guess that's the way it's supposed to be. But does it always work that way? Sometimes people's legal rights are denied, aren't they?"

"I'm sorry to say the answer is yes," Ms. Roth said. "But good lawyers, concerned judges, and responsible citizens are always trying to improve the system and make justice equal for everybody."

Jeff remembered reading the *Boys' Life* reprint on "Law and Justice." "Even the Greeks and Romans had systems of law," he said. "They took some of their ideas from the ancient Egyptians and Babylonians from thousands of years ago. Who knows, maybe even cavemen had some sort of system of laws."

**At the 1964 National Scout Jamboree, President Johnson told Scouts that the equality of all people—poor and rich—gives us all the right to enjoy liberty.**

"Cavemen! Aw, come on!" Marcus scoffed.

"Sure," replied Jeff. "When cavemen formed groups to help or protect each other, they made rules for behavior. The rules worked so everyone was satisfied. They kept the rules, and as time passed it was sort of a custom or tradition to obey the rules. So those could have been the first laws."

"As societies changed, as ways of living changed, laws also changed to meet new needs," said Ms. Roth. "Even today, new laws are needed and being made. That is one of the most important things to remember about law—it changes to develop effective solutions to new problems and new solutions to old problems."

WHAT IS LAW?

"That must mean lawyers have to keep a sharp lookout for new laws that they didn't learn when they were in school," said Marcus.

"That's absolutely right," Ms. Roth said. "There are a number of ways that new laws are made. Do any of you think you can name some?"

"In Washington, D.C., Congress passes bills that become law when the president signs them. That's called *legislation*," Marcus answered.

Ms. Roth said that was correct. "States also make laws. They have legislatures that make laws concerning the state and its citizens. Anyone can find these laws, called *statutes*, in large statute books. The statutes of the federal government are found in a set of large books called the *United States Code*."

"What gives state legislatures or the U.S. Congress the right to make laws?" asked one of the Scouts.

## Sources of Law

"Our Constitution is the supreme law of the United States. In that amazing document, the powers of Congress to make laws are set forth. It also gives states the power to legislate," Ms. Roth said.

Dig a little further to find the sources of law. Ask lawyers, judges, and your teachers. You will find many sources, such as tribal, customs, statutory (by legislation), constitutional, case, and common law.

During dinner, one of the Scouts brought up another source of law. This Scout recalled learning about the Ten Commandments and the various rules of behavior that developed from what is called *divine law*, or law issued directly from God.

"That's right," said Ms. Roth. "Every religion has some set of rules that are supposed to guide the way people live."

Marcus spoke up: "There are laws that punish a person who kills another person without justification. I guess you could trace the beginning of those laws all the way back to Moses and the Ten Commandments—maybe even further back."

Ms. Roth agreed: "Laws that are said to come from God were made a part of the beliefs and practices of various religions. When people started to write down laws to keep track of them, many religious laws were included."

"As time went on, societies developed laws based on social customs and religious and tribal laws," Ms. Roth said. "The U.S. legal system is a good example of a system that drew upon other systems to become what it is today. American law has its origins in English law, which in turn developed from certain concepts of Roman, Norman, and Germanic laws."

"Every society added something of its own to make the law fit special needs," said Raul.

WHAT IS LAW?

## The Patterns of Law

"Right," Ms. Roth said. "All the changes, additions, and years of development make the law work in a certain kind of way. Law always follows a pattern in its workings."

"I'm not sure I follow you, Ms. Roth," said Marcus with a puzzled look.

"Let me put it this way," Ms. Roth said. "Law is a way that helps people solve problems and disputes. Laws aren't made or decided just because somebody wants to do it his or her way. Judges, lawyers, and lawmakers follow guidelines—sort of a legal path or trail—to reach their decisions. This established procedure is one big reason why law helps keep order in society. Also, the decisions of a judge and the way a legislature works are usually open to public view. You can watch a courtroom trial and you can go to your state capitol, Washington, D.C., or even your local city or town council to observe how laws are followed or made."

"I'm still not sure what law means to me or my family," said Raul. "You've described what law is, but what does it do for me?"

Ms. Roth laughed. "Law affects all sorts of things concerning you and your family. For instance, a law in your state says that you must go to school when you reach a certain age and stay in school for a certain number of years. At the same time, law requires that your parents provide you with adequate food, clothing, and shelter up to a certain age."

Raul then asked, "Does the law control *everything?*"

"That's a good question," said Ms. Roth. "Some people think law should control more activities, and other people think law should control fewer."

Ms. Roth told the young men: "There is an old saying that the 'Law favors honor and order . . . life and liberty . . . and justice.' Finding out more about the law, how it works and what it does, is a real adventure. You should talk to your Scoutmaster and earn the Law merit badge."

"I know a lot more now than I did this morning," Jeff said. "You've gotten me interested in finding out as much as I can. When I get home, I'll talk to my Scoutmaster and he'll help me find a merit badge counselor. Maybe someday I'll be a lawyer, too!"

**Earning the Law merit badge will give you a good sense of how the law protects the rights of all citizens.**

= WHAT IS LAW?

Magna **CARTA**

Code of Hammurabi **MONOLITH**

Justinian **EMPEROR OF ROME**

# Great Beginnings: Where Law Comes From

Back home, one of the first things Jeff did was talk to his Scoutmaster about the Law merit badge. His Scoutmaster sent Jeff to the Law merit badge counselor, Mr. Hernandez.

They talked over the requirements and Mr. Hernandez promised to take Jeff to the courthouse to see the law in action. Then he suggested that Jeff start finding out where law comes from. "If you want to know where you are, you should know how you got there," Mr. Hernandez said.

He suggested that Jeff start his research at the public library or his school library to find out about the Code of Hammurabi, Justinian's Code, and the Magna Carta. Then, Mr. Hernandez said, Jeff should come back and tell him how parts of them apply today and show that he understood their main points.

Jeff told his parents at dinner that night: "It's really amazing that thousands of years ago the Babylonian people had written laws. And those laws developed from the law that other people lived under for centuries before that."

Jeff's mother suggested that he read what he'd written down at the library about early codes and the Magna Carta to practice what he would talk about with Mr. Hernandez.

## Early Codes and the Magna Carta

Jeff thought that was a good idea. He gathered his notes after dinner and read them to his parents. "Hammurabi was the king of the first Babylonian Empire. Because he ruled a large region with many kinds of people, he wanted to set up a system of law to apply everywhere in his empire," Jeff explained.

"The probability that we may fail in the struggle ought not to deter us from the support of a cause we believe to be just."

—Abraham Lincoln, 16th president of the United States, 1861–1865

## Great Beginnings: Where Law Comes From

"The Code of Hammurabi regulated trade inside and outside the empire, and recognized private property ownership. It divided the king's subjects into three classes: free citizens with full civil rights, ordinary citizens with fewer rights than free citizens, and slaves."

"The criminal law in the code made much use of the death penalty and often used cruel and drastic methods of punishment. If somebody hit and badly hurt another person, the offender's hand would be cut off!"

Jeff's father nodded. "That part about cutting off a person's hand for stealing or hurting someone reminds me of a Bible verse that talks about an eye for an eye and a tooth for a tooth."

The first thing Jeff found when he looked up Justinian's Code was another definition of law. In the sixth century, when Justinian was emperor of Rome, he said that law was "a theory of right and wrong" and "an art of the good and the equitable." Jeff thought that sounded very much like modern ideas of law.

The trouble in Rome more than 14 centuries ago was that its laws were an incredible mess! Roman laws were unclear to even the most intelligent people.

Jeff explained that the laws had to be untangled and collected so that they could be easily looked up. This process of collecting the laws and placing them in order by subject was called *codification*, from which we get the term *order of laws*. Justinian decided to form a committee of lawyers, judges, and wise citizens to place the laws into books. The committee arranged the laws into 50 books collectively called *The Digest*. Because the laws were updated and made understandable, people were more sure what the laws of their society were. Most important, people had a better chance for justice.

Justinian also made certain that his new code of law would not become old and useless. Periodically, new laws were published in books called *The Novels* to keep the code up to date.

Together, *The Digest* and *The Novels* formed the basis of civil law. Justinian's Roman laws greatly influenced the way law developed all over the Western world.

Jeff learned that one major contribution to the development of today's laws comes from England. In 1215, King John signed the Magna Carta, which means "great charter." It was a big step toward establishing English liberties and constitutional government. The Magna Carta in turn influenced American law in important ways.

> Even though the Magna Carta helped guarantee the rights for only a small number of free men who were lords, barons, knights, and rich landowners, it marked the beginning of written guarantees of people's rights. At that time most people were still feudal serfs—almost like slaves.

16  LAW

"At the start," Jeff said, "not everyone was included in the rights given by the U.S. Constitution. As time passed, more and more people were included."

"What do you mean by that?" asked Mr. Hernandez when Jeff visited him.

"When the United States was founded, only free white males who were property owners and at least 21 years old could vote. Later, the property requirement was dropped and all white adult males had the right to vote. In 1870, after the Civil War, former slaves were given the right to vote by the 15th Amendment to the Constitution," Jeff said.

"What about women during all that time?" Mr. Hernandez asked.

"Women finally could vote in 1920 when the 19th Amendment to the Constitution was adopted. American Indians were declared full citizens by law in 1924 and granted the right to vote. When the 26th Amendment passed in 1971, the vote was extended to anyone age 18 and older. These rights for everyone were a long time coming but they gradually became part of our law," Jeff told his counselor.

"The Magna Carta also gave rights only to free men at first, but when the feudal system ended and the present English system started to grow, more and more people were included."

**Abolitionist Frederick Douglass was a man ahead of his time. In addition to fighting for the rights of blacks, he also fought for the rights of women.**

## The Jury System

"You'll want to find out about the jury system next. A jury's role in trial has its origins in older systems, too," said Mr. Hernandez. "Find out how the jury became what it is today and explain what it does."

Jeff discovered two kinds of juries: *petit* or *petty jury*, which means small; and *grand jury*, which means large. A petit jury *deliberates*, or decides, the majority of criminal and civil cases. In most cases, 12 people are chosen to be members of a jury. These 12 jurors sit together to decide on the facts in a case and return a *verdict*—a decision about whether the person on trial is innocent or guilty of the charges against him or her.

A grand jury usually has more people than a petit jury. It also has a very different task. A grand jury meets privately to decide whether the government's lawyers can take an accused person to trial. The grand jury must consider evidence the government has gathered and then decide whether to *indict*, which means to accuse, a person. The government must offer proof to the grand jurors that a person suspected of a crime ought to go to trial.

> "Justice delayed is justice denied."
>
> —William Gladstone (1809–1898), four-time prime minister of Great Britain

Jeff found out that the jury has been a part of English and American law for hundreds of years. The jury system was brought to England around 1066. The idea was to get ordinary citizens who were not lawyers or judges involved in the legal system. The English jury system grew from other jury systems and took hundreds of years to evolve. There was a time, though, when there were no juries.

## Development of the Jury System

The first rather primitive jury system began in ancient Greece. Before a trial, a large number of citizens was chosen; then, just before a trial began, a smaller number was taken from the larger group. This was done so that no one could know ahead of time who would be a juror and try to influence the decision. Very often, hundreds of citizens would be on the jury. The very size of it made attempts to corrupt, bribe, or scare individual jurors difficult.

Imagine the confusion and noise of hundreds of people trying to decide important matters of property and even life and death! There were definitely faults in that system—but it was the first try.

The Romans gave the jury system a new shape. A judge defined the issues of a dispute, and a group of private persons called a *judice* made the decision on how to handle the problem. The *judices* (jurors) worked without a judge present. Their decisions were final and often harsh.

"Poor people who couldn't pay their debts were put in jail or even killed," Jeff told Mr. Hernandez.

The Romans decided that juries were too powerful and developed a trial system somewhat like ours—a hearing before a judge and a jury.

In early Germany, the head of the court would gather a small group of landowners to help decide cases. There were usually seven such helpers and sometimes 12. They could talk about the case away from the judge—much like the closed-door, secret discussions of American juries.

As people traveled across Europe, the idea of a jury spread. Norway, Sweden, and Denmark adopted juries. The jury system started in France when the invading Norsemen brought it with them. William the Conqueror brought the system to England in 1066 when he invaded the British Isles.

> "If we do not maintain justice, justice will not maintain us."
>
> —*Sir Francis Bacon (1561–1626), English philosopher*

After many years, the jury became a group that decided whether the facts of a case warranted an innocent or guilty verdict. Life was sometimes rough on those jurors. They were often locked in small rooms without food or drink until they reached a decision.

Jeff also learned that when English colonists came to America they brought the English system of law. The jury was an important part of that system and remained important in the colonies. It was seen as a way to keep the administration of justice in the hands of ordinary citizens and to prevent powerful or rich citizens from influencing the court.

## The Jury and U.S. Law

Among the first 10 amendments to the Constitution, known collectively as the Bill of Rights, are several that guarantee the right to a jury trial in federal criminal cases and certain civil cases. The Fourth, Fifth, Sixth, and Seventh Amendments are a package of rights that include a fair and speedy trial, the right to confront witnesses, the right to counsel (to have a lawyer), and the right to trial by jury in specified cases. The Fifth Amendment says that accused persons in criminal trials do not have to testify. These amendments, combined with statutes and *case law*—laws established by court decisions—make up the rights and procedures guaranteed to all Americans in court.

**The Bill of Rights**

Rules for jury trials are often different from state to state. Some states require unanimous verdicts or decisions. In other states, in trials for certain types of crimes, a verdict can come with 2/3, 3/4, or 5/6 of the jurors agreeing. Most states have juries of 12 people; others allow juries of fewer than 12.

Minor crimes such as traffic violations often do not have jury trials. "Just imagine the time it would take, the huge workload upon the justice system, if every person accused of speeding could have a jury trial," said Mr. Hernandez. "Still, any defendant going to trial may choose a jury trial."

Jeff wondered how juries were chosen. Mr. Hernandez explained that jury selection is usually accomplished by choosing names at random from voting lists. This method tends to ensure a mixture of jurors—men and women, poor and wealthy, people with different jobs and backgrounds. A juror should live in the area in which the crime allegedly took place and should have no criminal record. Lawyers for both sides may question possible jurors about their background and attitudes to see whether they should serve. Some possible jurors may be excused before the trial by the judge, and the lawyers can ask that certain jurors be excused if they display attitudes that might be harmful to their side of the case.

"Lawyers like to choose a jury that will be sympathetic to their side," Mr. Hernandez told Jeff. He went on to say that a possible juror must not know the people involved in the trial or have special feelings about them or the issues in the case.

Some critics question the effectiveness of juries. They say that jurors will not always follow a law they don't like or understand.

But those who favor the jury system praise its flexibility. They say that the jury realizes the spirit of the law and can shape true justice to a particular case. In reaching their decision, jurors try to apply a sense of fairness to the strict letter of the law.

## Location, Location, Location

If a defendant's lawyer feels a client might not receive a fair trial—because of pretrial publicity, for instance—the lawyer may request a *change of venue*. After reviewing the circumstances of the case, the appointed judge may or may not grant the motion to request a change of venue.

## Famous Trials

Mr. Hernandez gave Jeff the names of books that describe famous trials. (See the book list at the back of this pamphlet.)

"When you discover two trials that you would like to discuss with me, research the facts and issues and then prepare to tell me what was learned from each trial. Tell me what effect each trial had on life, liberty, and law," Mr. Hernandez instructed Jeff.

On the following pages are the two trials Jeff studied—the Trial of Socrates and the Nuremburg War Crimes Trials.

Other famous trials that you might want to look up include: *Gideon v. Wainwright,* decided in 1963 by the U.S. Supreme Court, which guaranteed a criminal defendant the assistance of an attorney if he or she cannot afford one; and *Sheppard v. Maxwell,* decided by the Supreme Court in 1966, which involved a conflict between two of our most important rights—freedom of the press and the right to a fair trial.

**Prosecutor Ralph Albrecht addresses the Nuremberg court in 1945.**

# The Trial of Socrates:
## *The right to be different, to think freely, and to speak your opinions.*

Socrates was a philosopher—a thinker and teacher—who lived in Athens in ancient Greece. His ideas were unpopular with the rulers of Athens.

Socrates believed that goodness is based on knowledge, and wickedness on ignorance. He tried to teach people the meaning of his motto Know Thyself and to open their minds to new thoughts. He always searched for truth and never hesitated to criticize the government and its leaders. Because they feared and hated him, the government leaders arrested Socrates and put him on trial for "corruption of the young" and "neglect of the gods whom the city worships."

Most of the jury of 500 men disagreed with Socrates and his defense of freedom of speech and thought. He had no lawyer to assist him.

Because the truth often hurts when it uncovers dishonesty, evil people sometimes want to stamp out the free exchange of ideas. Socrates did not convince the jury of his innocence and was condemned to death by swallowing poison. He spent his last hours of life talking over his ideas with friends. He took the poison and died peacefully, with the knowledge that the truth will never die.

**Greek philosopher Socrates once said, "Nothing is to be preferred before justice."**

# The Nuremberg War Crimes Trials:
## *Conscience, morality, and the state.*

During World War II the Nazi government of Germany set out to conquer Europe. In the process, millions of people were thrown into the horrors of war. Huge numbers of soldiers on all sides died in the long, bloody combat.

Millions of innocent civilians—men, women, and children—were deliberately put to death by the Nazis. These deaths were not unavoidable, accidental, or battle-connected: They were planned mass murders carried out as part of the Nazis' insane quest to produce a "master race." The main group of civilian victims were 6 million European Jews, who were starved, shot, or fed into gas chambers and fiery furnaces. This number included more than 1 million children. Soldiers who were prisoners of the Nazis also were executed. Millions of innocent people died.

When the war ended in 1945, the victorious Allies—United States, Britain, and Russia—were shocked at the Nazi crimes. Many nations had long agreed to obey certain laws—rules of war—that would keep civilians out of violence and danger as much as possible, and would treat prisoners of war humanely.

The Nazis violated all such rules of war. Worse, they violated rules of humanity, decency, and morality. The Allies put Nazi officials, generals, admirals, and private citizens on trial in Nuremberg, Germany, for their crimes against humanity.

A panel of judges from many nations decided that people could not abandon their basic humanity even if the government says they must. The court also ruled that a government that orders the killing and torture of innocent people is acting outside the law and thereby loses its right to govern.

The principles of decency and human rights for all were affirmed by the Nuremberg War Crimes Trials. Many Nazi war criminals were executed or imprisoned. Other Nazis killed themselves when they realized their positions were indefensible in law or morality.

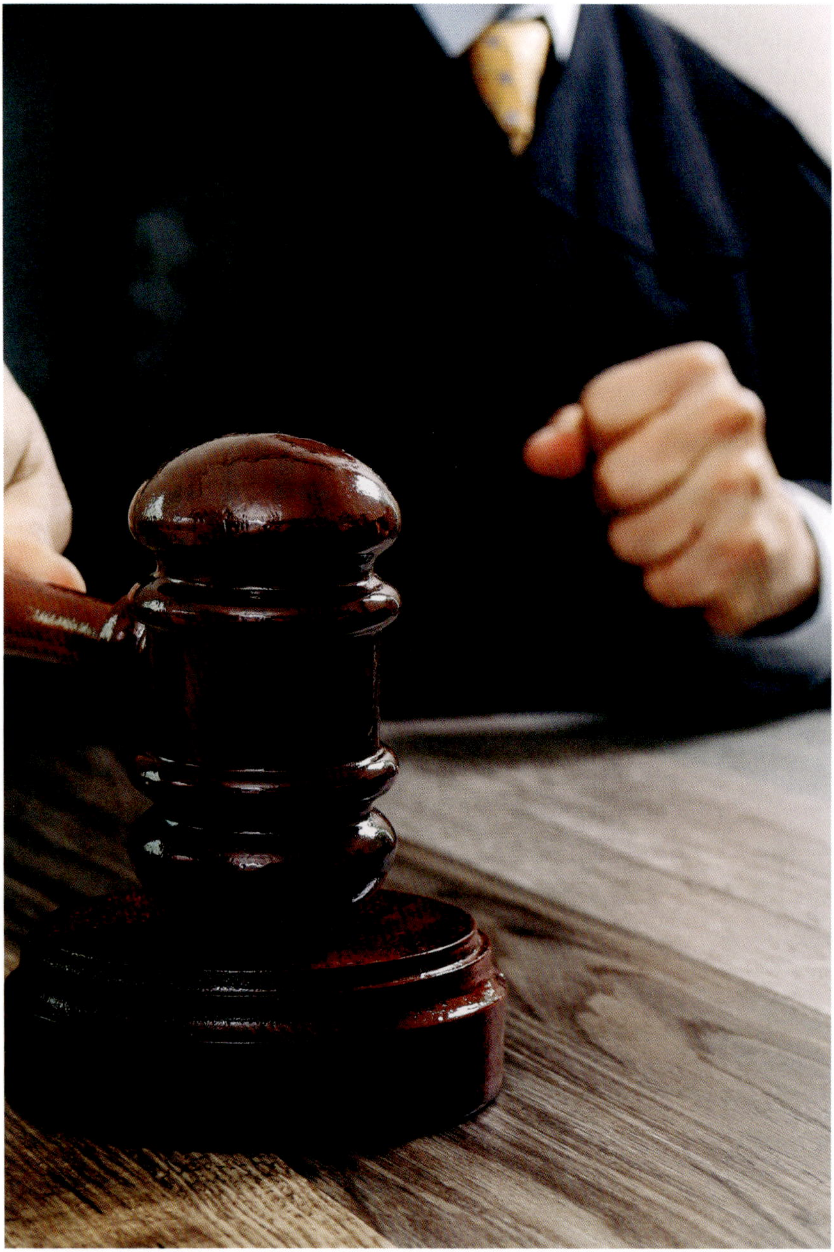

# Civil and Criminal Law

Jeff learned that there are two separate systems of solving legal disputes—civil law and criminal law. Disagreements between two parties about their rights and responsibilities are handled in *civil actions*. They involve the private and civil rights of individuals, corporations, government bodies, and others.

Criminal law is concerned with harmful acts called *crimes*. Crimes are forbidden by statute law, and if the person who commits a crime is discovered, the state will take that person to court and seek punishment in the name of the people.

To keep the basic concepts of civil and criminal law clear in his mind, Jeff made the following chart:

|  | CRIMINAL LAW | CIVIL LAW |
| --- | --- | --- |
| **WHO IS INVOLVED** | The state prosecutes; it goes to court against the accused person. | Usually a person or corporation goes to court against another person or corporation. |
| **THE "BURDEN OF PROOF"** | The state must prove the accused person is guilty "beyond a reasonable doubt." | The plaintiff must prove its position by a "preponderance of the evidence." |
| **PENALTIES** | Imprisonment and/or a fine. | No imprisonment. An award of money (called "damages") or an order to perform or refrain from performing an act is issued. |

What does Jeff's chart tell us? You probably can think of quite a few crimes. But did you know that civil law is the "bigger" of the two kinds? More people are involved with civil law than with criminal law, and more civil law cases are decided in courts. But you probably have heard more about criminal cases than you have heard about the thousands of civil cases that wind their way through the courts each day.

## Civil Law

Today's civil law developed from Roman civil law. It is the branch of the law that affects all citizens and a wide range of rights and legal questions. While criminal law deals with wrongs committed against the public, civil law deals with wrongs committed against individuals.

A civil action may seek to recover money or property that rightfully belongs to someone, or to correct a situation a person thinks is wrong, unfair, or unjust.

Civil law remedies arguments over private rights. The people seeking a remedy are *adversary parties*. That simply means that one person is on one side of an argument and someone else is on the other side. The one bringing the suit is called the *plaintiff*. The one charged with doing something wrong is the *defendant*.

Jeff made a list of things that civil law includes.

Civil law includes:

- Contracts
- Corporation law
- Marriage
- Divorce
- Trusts
- Wills
- Estates
- Patents
- Copyrights
- Trademarks
- Taxes
- Property (land, buildings, money, jewelry, and so forth)
- Torts

From that long list, Jeff discovered that most civil law cases arise from contracts and torts. But what are torts? A *tort* is a wrong or an injury committed against persons or property other than a breach of contract. Examples include trespass, false arrest, libel, slander, negligence, nuisance, and assault and battery. If people camp on posted land without permission, they may have committed the tort of trespass. The owner of the property might start a civil action against the trespasser and ask for money, which is referred to as "damages," or other relief.

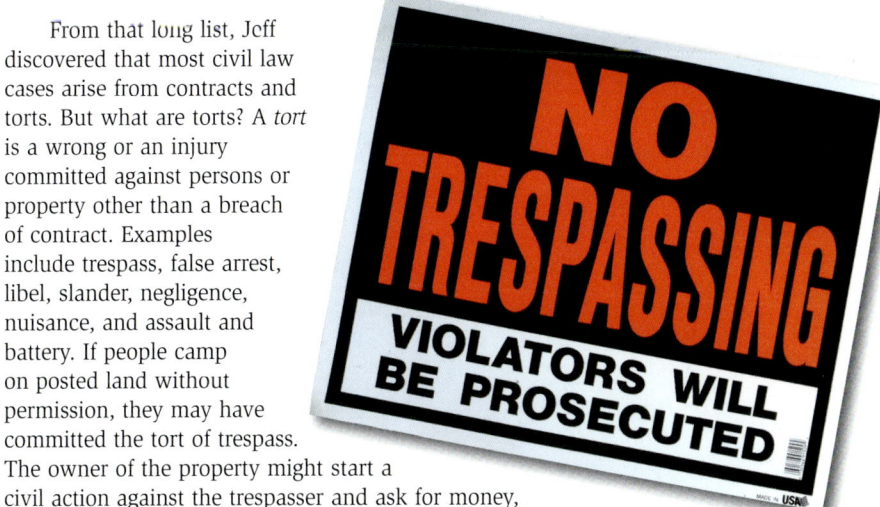

## Criminal Law

Look at Jeff's chart again as you make comparisons between civil and criminal law. You will see that criminal law leaves the responsibility of enforcing and prosecuting largely to the government. The government will act as plaintiff and prosecute the accused, asking for punishment in the name of the people. The accused in this criminal action becomes the defendant. Thus, while civil law protects private rights, criminal law involves the protection of us all.

People who are accused of breaking criminal laws are protected by law, too. The U.S. Constitution and state constitutions assure persons of many rights and safeguards in the criminal law process. The right to a lawyer, even if the defendant cannot pay for one, and the right to a fair and speedy trial (by jury if the defendant wishes) are basic rights of accused persons.

Some crimes, of course, are far more serious than others. Crimes are divided into two categories: felonies and misdemeanors. A *misdemeanor* is a crime that usually results in a fine or a penalty of no more than one year's imprisonment. *Felonies* carry greater punishments, usually imprisonment in a state penitentiary. A forcible felony, such as murder, rape, robbery, burglary, arson, kidnapping, or any other felony that involves the use or threat of physical violence, carries long jail terms.

# Types of Crimes

**Offenses Against a Person**
1. Homicide (murder, manslaughter, and reckless homicide)
2. Assault and battery; aggravated assault (placing a person in fear of bodily harm and causing bodily harm)
3. Kidnapping (confinement of another person against his or her will)
4. Robbery (theft from a person by force or threat of force)

**Offenses Against Property**
1. Burglary (breaking and entering with intent to commit a felony or theft)
2. Arson (damage done deliberately by fire or explosives)
3. Larceny (taking away property without the owner's consent and with the intent to permanently deprive the owner)
4. Embezzlement (fraudulent use and appropriation of property or money entrusted to a person by others)
5. Theft (obtaining control of property by deception or threat)
6. Fraud (taking property by false pretenses)
7. Receiving, concealing, or selling stolen property
8. Forgery (making or altering any document or using such document to knowingly defraud)
9. Counterfeiting (copying money or documents to deceive or defraud)
10. Extortion (obtaining money or valuable property by threat or force)

**Other Crimes**
1. Hijacking of boats, airplanes, trains, automobiles, and buses
2. Unlawful use of a weapon
3. Illegal eavesdropping

= CIVIL AND CRIMINAL LAW

Within these two categories, criminal law has natural divisions. Crimes can be committed against a person, against property, and in other ways.

Jeff went to the law library at the county courthouse to find out more. Mr. Hernandez had told Jeff to pick any state in the whole country and any crime. Then he should look up that state's *criminal code*—its criminal laws—for that crime.

State criminal codes can also be found online by searching for your state and "criminal code."

Jeff picked a thick, red book with gold letters. It was the *Illinois Revised Statutes.* He checked the index and opened the volume to the section on the Illinois Criminal Code. He looked for the code on armed robbery, and made copies of a few pages so he could take them with him. Later, after reading those pages, he had a discussion with his counselor.

"Imagine this," Mr. Hernandez said. "You are walking down the street and suddenly a man points a gun at your head and tells you to hand over your money fast. After handing over your money, the gunman tries to get away as quickly as possible. If that happened, what laws would have been broken?"

LAW 31

Jeff thought for a moment. "Stealing! He stole my money."

"The law is much more exact than that," Mr. Hernandez said. "Every crime has its proper category. Look at sections 18.1 and 18.2 of the Illinois Criminal Code. Read it to me."

Jeff looked up the sections and read aloud.

"'A person commits robbery when he or she takes property . . . from the person or presence of another by the use of force or by threatening the imminent use of force.' So that would have been a robbery, right?"

"Read on," Mr. Hernandez said.

"'A person commits armed robbery when he or she violates section 18.1, and he or she carries on or about his or her person or is otherwise armed with a firearm,'" Jeff read.

"There you have it," said Mr. Hernandez. "Robbery is what the law calls a Class 2 felony. Armed robbery is a far more serious crime. The law says armed robbery 'is a Class X felony for which 15 years shall be added to the term of imprisonment imposed by the court.'"

"What about this 'burden of proof' business?" asked Jeff.

"That means that in a criminal law case, the state can hope to get a *conviction*—a finding of guilty—against the accused *only* if guilt is proven 'beyond a reasonable doubt.'"

"How is that different from 'preponderance of the evidence' in civil law?"

"In civil law, your proof and evidence must be the most believable and give more of a feeling of truth than the other party can give. In criminal law, you are concerned with a person's liberty, not just money. 'Beyond a reasonable doubt' means that the state must fully satisfy the jury so that jurors are entirely convinced of the defendant's guilt. The evidence presented must be absolutely clear, precise, and certain. There just cannot be any room for doubt when a person's freedom is at stake."

"Do you think it's always smart to put convicted criminals in jail?" Jeff asked.

"Jail can be a very rough, horrible experience. Many judges realize that the prison system needs a lot of attention and reform, so they won't put certain people in prison."

"What else can they do?"

= Civil and Criminal Law

"They can place an offender on probation. Especially for younger, first-time offenders, jail might do more harm than good. *Probation* means that the offender will be under the supervision of the court. A probation officer will meet with the offender from time to time. The offender may be allowed to live at home and lead a normal life, but with restrictions on where he or she can go, what he or she can do, and whom he or she can see. The offender must check in with the probation officer and must stay out of trouble. At any sign or hint that the offender is violating a law or restriction, the probation could be ended and the supervising judge might send the person to jail. Probation is a way of giving someone a second chance."

"What about people already in jail? Do they have any chance to show the community that they will not break the law again?"

"Yes, Jeff. The legal system is based on the belief that justice and mercy go together. A person in jail may be entitled to parole after having served a certain portion of the prison term. If the offender behaves in jail and shows that he or she truly has changed, learned from past mistakes (the crime committed), and will not be a danger to society, a group of citizens called a parole board may decide to release him or her before the sentence is completed."

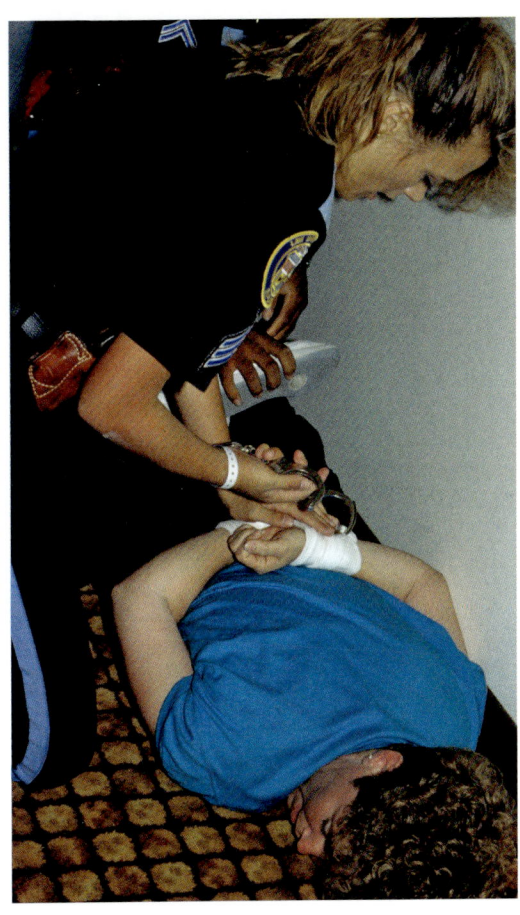

LAW   33

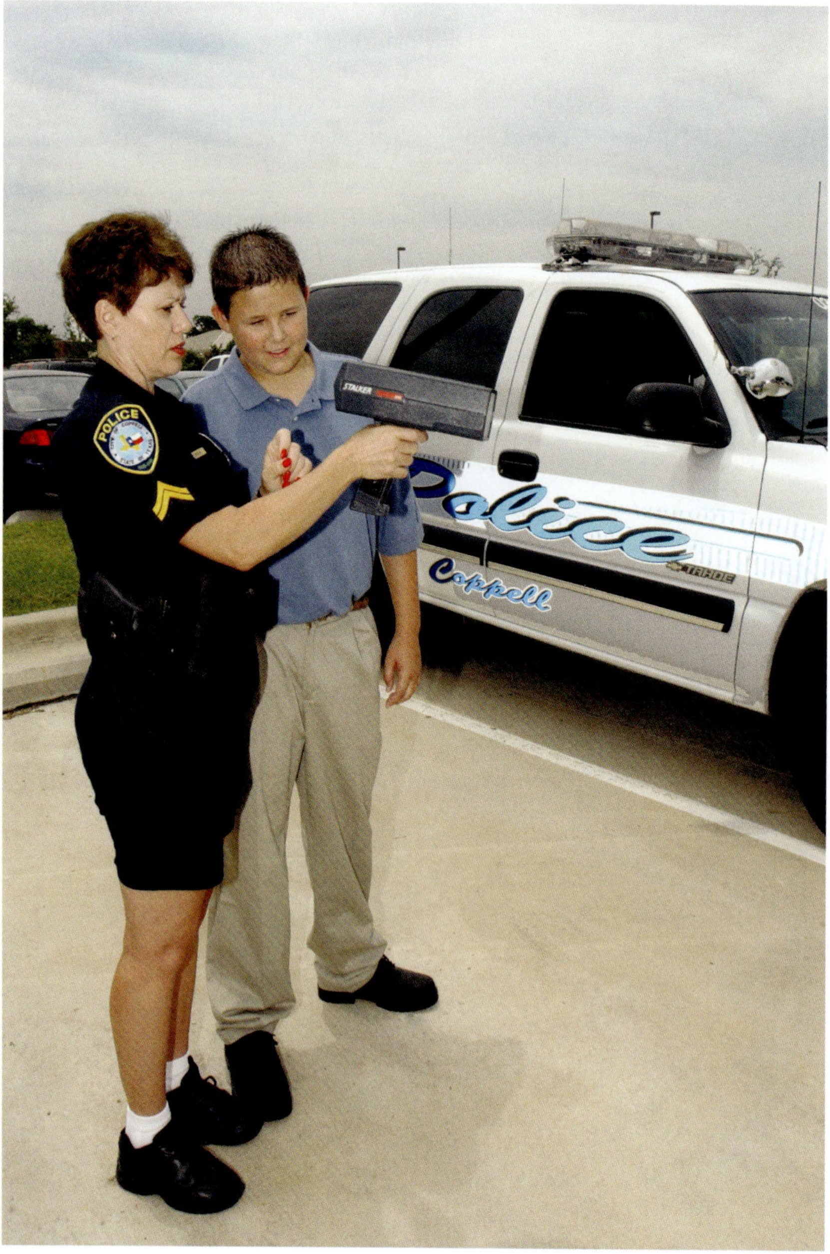
POLICE
STALKER
Police
Coppell
TAHOE

# Law Enforcement: More Than a Gun and a Badge

Jeff was ready to begin requirement 4. He was eager to learn about the responsibilities of local police or sheriff's departments and the state and national law enforcement agencies.

Jeff was aware that police often are considered the first line of defense in the legal system. Society would most likely be chaotic without police protection and services.

"Even though the police serve necessary functions of enforcing criminal laws, protecting lives and property, and maintaining order, many people resent them," Mr. Hernandez said. "Some members of society view the police as a harsh tool of a system that has deprived and hurt them. Police officers sometimes find their own prejudices aroused and return that distrust. As a result, the police and the people they are supposed to serve sometimes don't get along."

"It must be very hard to be a police officer," Jeff said quietly. He knew about the mixed feelings toward police. He knew that police do good things, too. (For help in getting people's views on law enforcement, see the questionnaire later in this chapter.)

Jeff made an appointment and went to the district police station near his home to talk to Corporal Deborah O'Brien. "Hello, Jeff," she said as they shook hands. "I'm the watch commander this afternoon. That means I have to keep an eye on all the patrols during this shift, so why don't we sit in the communications room."

LAW ENFORCEMENT: MORE THAN A GUN AND A BADGE

Corporal O'Brien and Jeff entered a large room full of electronic equipment, lighted maps of the town, and other devices. The lighted maps were "crime maps" and patrol area maps showing where patrol cars were and where extra patrols cars were needed to help prevent crimes.

Jeff watched the lighted panels and heard the crackling of radio messages coming to the station from patrol officers. He told Corporal O'Brien about his conversation with Mr. Hernandez.

## The Role of the Law Enforcement Officer

The corporal looked serious and spoke slowly. "It is almost impossible to take care of every problem. But being a police officer means handling problems. We have to protect lives and property, of course, and we try to detect crime and arrest offenders. Police officers must also handle unruly crowds, patrol streets, protect neglected or lost children, give emergency first aid, step into family arguments, among other things.

36   LAW

"Most police departments send their officers through some sort of training institute. This is rarely enough to train officers to cope with complex problems, different groups of people, and various situations."

"What does this department do to educate its police officers better?" Jeff asked.

"Our officers take college courses on department time and at the department's expense. We hope our personnel can learn as much as possible about people and problem solving. We want to make this police force more professional. It is important for an officer to understand people and society by learning about sociology and psychology," Corporal O'Brien said.

Another way to increase police professionalism is to eliminate improper conduct. Jeff wondered what citizens can do if they have complaints against a police officer or the department.

Corporal O'Brien explained: "Most departments have either a civilian review board or an internal complaints section. A group of citizens or the department itself may investigate if a complaint has merit. If a police officer is found to be responsible for the action charged in the complaint, he or she can be fired or suspended for a period of time without pay. Of course, if the officer committed a criminal act, he or she can be prosecuted."

She continued: "Police officers would like to see crime reduced and prevented. A good place to start is with young people. When young people get in trouble with the law, they need special guidance. This department, like many others, has special officers who work with young people only. They are called juvenile officers. It is their duty to talk to young people and try to help them stay out of trouble with the law. Prison is no place for anyone to be. We try to see to it that as few youths as possible end up in that miserable situation."

"How do you become a police officer?" asked Jeff.

"We give interested applicants a written examination to test their intelligence and mental alertness," Corporal O'Brien said. "They also get a physical agility test. The highest scoring candidates will be the first ones asked to take further tests as jobs open up in the department. Candidates must have good character and no criminal convictions. We check their backgrounds very carefully. They also must have at least a high school diploma or the equivalent. After formal training at a police institute, new officers spend time on patrol duty with an experienced patrol officer. Only then do they become full-fledged police officers."

## Problems of Law Enforcement

Corporal O'Brien lifted a large book with very wide pages and placed it on the table in front of Jeff. "Now, you can take a look at exactly what a law enforcement officer does during a typical day. This is called our log. The *log* tells what each officer on patrol did while on duty."

Jeff looked through the log and saw many examples of police officers protecting lives and property. One officer gave first aid at a car crash, and another helped settle a family argument.

As Jeff leafed through more pages in the police log, he counted many citations for speeding, failing to stop at a stop sign, and other traffic violations.

Corporal O'Brien noted that many policemen are bothered that they must do certain tasks that people with less training could probably do. "Desk and clerk work, minor traffic violations, traffic control, and court appearances drain time and personnel from the police force. Hundreds of hours are lost by sitting in court or writing traffic tickets. 'Para-police' or community service officers—civilians who provide assistance to police but aren't authorized to arrest people—could handle some of these duties, freeing well-trained law enforcement officers to spend more time patrolling, preventing crime, and working with youth."

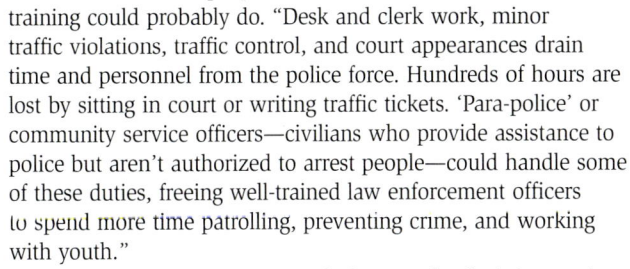

Jeff thought that was a good idea. He thanked Corporal O'Brien for her time and interest. "I really have a better idea now of what law enforcement is all about."

> The following questionnaire will help you find out more about people's attitudes toward law enforcement officials and their work. The questionnaire does not reflect any views of the Boy Scouts of America. Rather, it tries to raise issues so that a wide range of opinions and ideas can be discussed.

## Sample Questions to Ask the General Public for Requirement 4

With these questions, interview people to find out their views. After they answer these questions, discuss your views with them.

After they answer these questions, discuss their views with them.

1. What role do law enforcement officers play in protecting the citizens and the property in your community?
2. What recommendations would you make for improving relations between law enforcement officers and citizens in your community?
3. If you had an opportunity to speak to a law enforcement officer, what questions would you ask?
4. In your opinion, how can we help law enforcement?

# Sample Questions to Ask Law Enforcement Officers for Requirement 4

Discuss the questions below with a law enforcement officer. Probe the officer's attitudes toward the job he or she holds and the public he or she serves. Your conversation should cover a wide range of topics, some of which might not be mentioned here.

1. In your opinion, what are your duties and responsibilities to your community?

2. What training and education did you receive in order to be a law enforcement officer?

3. How can we help you do a better job? Do you want the public's help? How can people and the police understand each other better?

4. What is being done in your community to help police officers and people know each other better? How does diversity in your community affect your job? What else can be done to help officers know the community?

5. What are the biggest crime problems in our area? How do police deal with these problems?

## State and Federal Law Enforcement

Besides local law enforcement agencies such as the police, Jeff learned about state and federal law enforcement agencies.

The enforcement of state laws is often the duty of the state police. State troopers patrol state and interstate highways for traffic violators and arrest criminal suspects within the state. Large rural areas and many small towns often lack effective police protection. Small forces are often underequipped, understaffed, and undertrained.

Federal government agencies such as the Federal Bureau of Investigation have law enforcement responsibilities. The FBI investigates violations of federal law. Activities that threaten the peace and security of the United States also are under FBI jurisdiction. The FBI is a branch of the U.S. Department of Justice. FBI agents are college educated and often have legal training. They receive special training in law enforcement and crime detection at the FBI Academy. Jeff also remembered Corporal O'Brien telling him that the FBI helps local and state law enforcement agencies by maintaining a central file of millions of fingerprints.

"Police work means more than I ever thought it did," Jeff told his parents. "Law enforcement deals with many problems in our society, which is far from perfect and needs everyone's help."

## Laws That Help Protect Consumers and Sellers

Jeff turned his attention to requirement 5. He wanted to learn more about laws that help protect buyers and sellers. He looked up the Federal Trade Commission on the internet and found the Bureau of Consumer Protection's Division of Enforcement at www.ftc.gov/about-ftc/bureaus-offices.

He learned that the Bureau's enforcement division conducts a wide variety of law enforcement activities to protect consumers. These include conducting investigations and prosecuting civil actions to stop fraudulent, unfair, or deceptive marketing and advertising practices; and enforcing consumer protection laws, rules, and guidelines.

Jeff discovered that this important arm of law enforcement has recently investigated e-commerce and the internet, including online shopping and unfulfilled holiday delivery promises. It also handles complaints about employment opportunities fraud. These "consumer cops" often check into scholarship scams that falsely guarantee scholarships.

The Bureau of Consumer Protection investigates questionable claims about the safety and effectiveness of diet drugs, weight loss aids, herbal remedies, and alternative treatments. Advertisers who make false claims about these products may come under the scrutiny of the Bureau's officers, which could result in action before federal administrative law judges or the U.S. District Courts.

The Bureau enforces trade laws, rules, and guides through administrative or federal court proceedings. Such rules include the Mail or Telephone Order Merchandise Rule, which requires regular and online companies to ship purchases to consumers when promised (or within 30 days if no time is specified) or to give consumers the option to cancel their order for a refund.

If a company sells a T-shirt with a "Made in U.S.A." label, it must comply with the Bureau's guidelines for making that claim. Another trade rule helps protect consumers from fraud by requiring fiber content labeling of textile, wool, and fur products, with care label instructions attached to clothing and fabrics.

Other energy rules require companies to disclose the energy costs of home appliances, the octane ratings of gasoline, and the efficiency rating of home insulation.

## Fraud

When Jeff told his counselor what he had learned about consumer protection laws, Mr. Hernandez nodded his approval. "You know, Jeff, a major problem facing Americans today is fraud," Mr. Hernandez said.

"What exactly is fraud?" Jeff asked.

Jeff's counselor explained that *fraud* means that a false statement—a lie—must be spoken, acted, or written, and the person making the false statement must know it is untrue when it is made. This act of fraud can sometimes make a binding contract between two people invalid or unenforceable. The falsehood must have influenced the person who was deceived and misled, so that money or other property was lost because he or she believed and relied upon that statement.

Mr. Hernandez suggested that Jeff think about the following examples: "If a real estate broker sells land to a buyer, promising that this is the richest, most fertile farmland in the region, but it turns out the land is sand and you can't grow a single potato on it, is the seller guilty of fraud? Or could you say that the seller was only stating an opinion to help sell that land?"

Jeff thought for a moment. "You know, the buyer doesn't have to take the broker's word. The buyer can observe the land and check things out."

Mr. Hernandez agreed. "That's what is meant by the old saying Buyer Beware! But what if someone applied for a life insurance policy and concealed past medical problems from the insurance company? Is this concealment an effort to obtain the policy by fraud? Do these examples fit into the definition of fraud?"

"That's a good question!" Jeff said. "I'll think about it."

## Spirit of Fairness

The law recognizes that bargains made between buyers and sellers must have a spirit of fairness and an element of basic justice. *Gross overreaching* means taking obvious unfair advantage of a weaker party in a contract. Such unethical practices are not tolerated by some courts. Mr. Hernandez gave an example of a situation in which a consumer agreed to a contract that appeared to be unfair.

In a case titled *Williams v. Walker-Thomas Furniture Co.*, which was decided in the mid 60s, Ms. Williams bought furniture and appliances over time from the furniture company. She bought about $1,800 worth of goods and owed the company about $200. "You might think she owned what she had already paid for," Mr. Hernandez said.

But she did not. Each time Ms. Williams bought new items from the company, she signed a complicated contract that said until full payment was made for all the items she had ever bought there, those items belonged to the store. If she missed one of her payments, the store would repossess, or take back, every single piece. The store knew that she was out of work and that she supported herself and her seven children on a $218 monthly check from the government.

She bought another item and missed the first payment. The store took everything back—more than $1,600 worth of goods already paid for were gone because Ms. Williams had signed a contract full of fine print and technical, hard-to-understand language. She understood, however, that something unfair was happening to her.

Ms. Williams went to court to challenge the legality of the contract. The trial judge said that because she had signed the contract, she was bound to responsibilities under the agreement. If it was unfair, she should have refused to sign it.

Ms. Williams and her lawyer appealed to the U.S. Court of Appeals. Judge J. Skelly Wright reviewed the case. He reversed the decision of the trial judge and decided that there are times when a contract's terms are shocking to decency—"unconscionable," he called it. He said that Ms. Williams's contract was so full of unreasonable, deceptive, hidden language that she had no idea what she was signing. The court, he went on, should not allow such things by approving them as legal.

Jeff was impressed with Judge Wright's logic and humane attitude. "The law wouldn't be respected by everybody if it allowed such things to go on. I'm glad there are judges like Judge Wright!"

Mr. Hernandez continued, "A good judge, no matter if he or she presides over a local traffic court or the Supreme Court, will always try to combine the strict letter of the law with the spirit of the law."

## Consumer Protection

Mr. Hernandez also told Jeff about the **Truth in Lending Act,** which was passed in 1968 as part of the **Consumer Protection Act**. This set of laws requires the seller to inform the buyer in clear terms exactly how much interest will be charged for a loan or credit agreement. Laws that enforce truth in labeling, packaging, and advertising also help. The Federal Trade Commission, the Food and Drug Administration, and even the Federal Communications Commission have all taken steps to help protect American consumers.

Mr. Hernandez said: "You can easily research these agencies on the internet. Just access www.ftc.gov, www.fda.gov, or www.fcc.gov and you will learn a great deal."

When Jeff got home that night, he read more about various acts on the Federal Trade Commission's website. Here is what he learned about some laws that were passed to protect consumers.

> Always have a parent's permission before using the internet.

The **Children's Online Privacy Protection Act of 1998** protects young people's privacy by giving parents the tools to control what information is collected from their children online. Commercial website and online services operators who knowingly collect personal information from children under age 13 must

- Notify parents.
- Obtain parental consent before collecting data on the child.
- Give parents a choice as to whether their child's information will be disclosed to third parties.
- Provide parents with access to their child's information.
- Let parents prevent further use of collected information.
- Not require a child to provide more information than is reasonably necessary to participate in an activity.
- Maintain the "confidentiality, security, and integrity of the information."

Another emerging area of consumer law deals with *identity theft*. What is identity theft? It happens when someone exploits the use of your name, Social Security number, credit card number, or some other personal information without your knowledge and with the intent to commit fraud or theft. One way for someone to steal another's identity is through a *phishing scam*. This involves sending an email that claims to be from a financial institution or a government agency asking you to verify personal information. The message directs you to a website that looks official but isn't. To protect yourself, never email personal or financial information. The **Identity Theft and Assumption Deterrence Act of 1998** makes the Federal Trade Commission (FTC) a central clearinghouse for identity theft complaints. The act requires the FTC to log and acknowledge such complaints, provide victims with relevant information, and refer their complaints to appropriate agencies and law enforcement.

## The FTC, the Web, and You

One area that concerns the Federal Trade Commission is the protection of children who use the internet. The FTC's Children's Online Privacy Protection Act of 1998 calls for operators of commercial websites and online services to "obtain verifiable consent from a parent or guardian before they collect personal information from children."

There are laws that help protect consumers from being harassed by aggressive telemarketers and other advertisers.

# Organizations That Help Protect Consumers and Sellers

When Jeff and Mr. Hernandez met again, Jeff told his counselor about some of the acts he'd learned more about at the Federal Trade Commission's website.

Mr. Hernandez told Jeff it was important to remember that state and local governments also have a department of consumer affairs and laws to help victims of fraud and dishonest business practices.

For example, the **Illinois Consumer Fraud and Deceptive Business Practices Act** protects people who have been talked into buying things they don't need by high-pressure door-to-door salespeople. The law says that a person can cancel an order for an item he or she agreed to buy within three days of the sale if the total cost is more than $25. Many states have consumer fraud acts that regulate retail sales, and make the consumer and seller share the cost of repairs for certain parts on used cars.

Many local and county governments also have an office which handles fraud, consumer complaints, fair business practices, and consumer protection. If people don't report their complaints to such agencies, however, the agencies can't be useful. Honest businesspeople benefit when dishonest ones are taken to court. Everyone benefits when fraud is prosecuted in court.

Small claims courts exist to settle legal disputes over relatively small amounts of money or property. These courts also help the consumer. Legal aid organizations and public defender offices help people who cannot afford a lawyer.

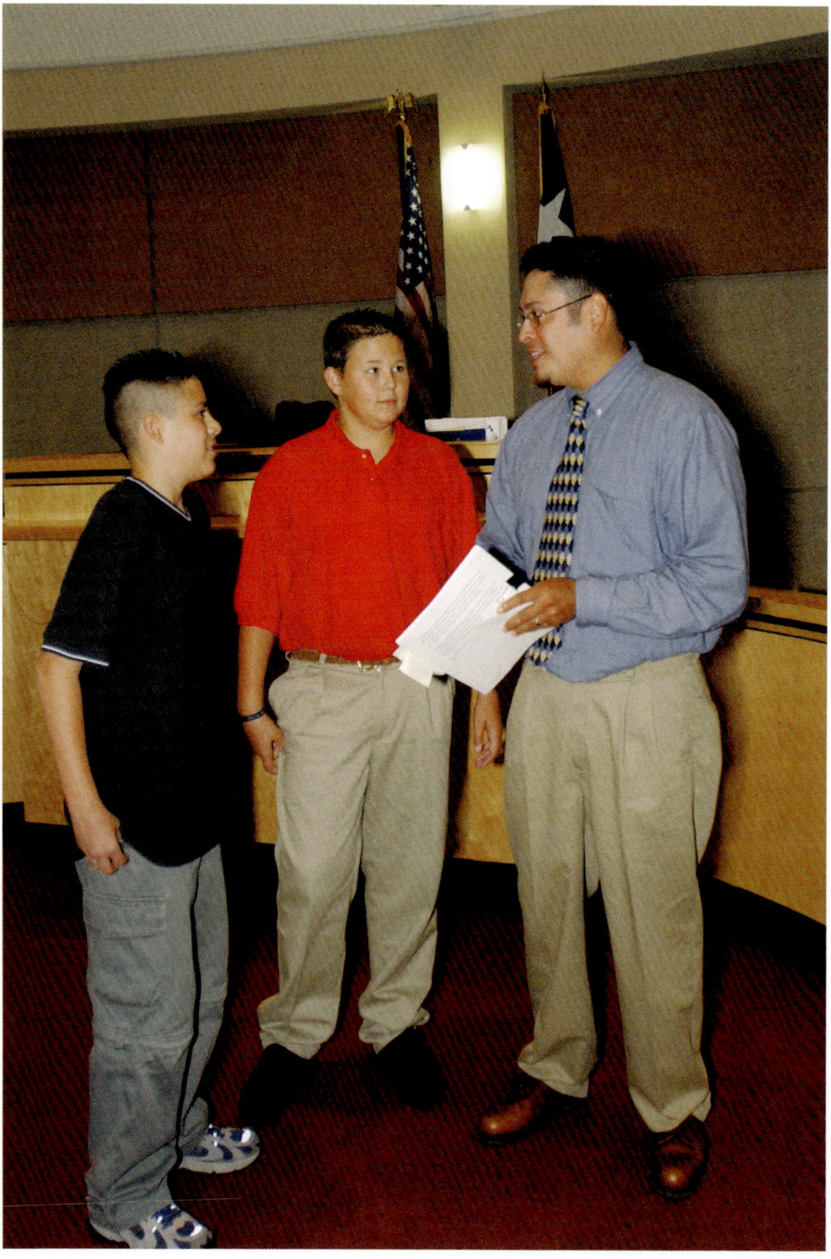

# The Law in Action

Jeff was now ready to visit a courtroom so he could see the law in action. He invited his friend Raul to join him and Mr. Hernandez. Before they left, Mr. Hernandez thought it would be a good idea to talk about what they would see and hear. He, Jeff, and Raul decided to go first to a civil trial that involved the tort of negligence. Negligence is a large area within the law of torts and it accounts for many cases in civil courts across the country.

"Just what is negligence?" Jeff asked.

"That's a big question," Mr. Hernandez said. "Negligence can be confusing to some people—even lawyers. Let's begin by saying that *negligence* is a failure to do something that a reasonable person, guided by ordinary considerations, would do. Or, it's doing something that a reasonable and prudent person would not do."

"I'm not sure I'm following you," Jeff said.

"Look at it this way," said his counselor. "Negligence usually involves thoughtlessness, carelessness, and inattention to the interests and safety of other people. You will see this definition in action when you go to court."

Mr. Hernandez explained to them that there are degrees of negligence. If someone acts to put another person in fear or actual danger, that willful kind of behavior is "wanton" and "reckless" and is often called *gross negligence*. It is an act or failure to act when one has the duty to act. The act can be dangerous or careless. In some cases, what is *not* done can be just as dangerous.

"Maybe if you could give us an example, it would help us understand better," Jeff said.

## The Law in Action

"Suppose a construction company makes a hole in a public sidewalk to connect a new building to underground pipes. The builder doesn't cover the hole at night or put up a warning sign. A person walking along in the dark could fall into that hole and get seriously hurt. The law of negligence asks if the builder is responsible to warn passersby of that danger," explained Mr. Hernandez.

"That seems careless to me," Raul said.

"But what if the passerby knew it was a construction area and knew such holes might exist? Isn't that person assuming the risk of walking in what is known to be a dangerous area?"

"Hmmm . . . I didn't think of that," Raul admitted.

"In some states, tort law makes it clear that a duty of care and protection is owed," Mr. Hernandez said. "In other states, the plaintiff's lawyer must establish the defendant's duty.

"The question of duty in this construction hole case is unclear. The plaintiff's lawyer will try to prove that a duty was owed to the person who fell into the hole."

The rules of civil procedure see to it that each side has an equal chance to present its case as fully and as well as possible. Hopefully, this method is fair to weak and strong parties alike. In addition, the contesting parties bear the burden of time, effort, and energy to solve their controversy. Unlike criminal cases, the state is not a party to a civil matter.

## A Trial Involving Negligence

The next day Jeff and Raul went to the U.S. District Court to sit in on the case of *Tompkins v. Southern Airways*. They learned that Ms. Tompkins was a passenger on a Southern Airways DC-9 jet flying from Nashville to Dallas. Near Dallas, the plane was flying at about 4,000 feet when the pilot suddenly saw a U.S. Air Force plane about a half mile away.
The planes were on a collision course. Without warning, the pilot of the DC-9 pushed the plane into a steep, 500-foot dive to pass under the Air Force plane. In the sudden dive, Ms. Tompkins was thrown from her seat and injured. Ms. Tompkins sued the airline for $25,000 in a negligence action.

## THE LAW IN ACTION

As the lawyer for Ms. Tompkins explained, a negligence tort has several elements that must be proven to win the suit. First, the lawyer must prove that the defendant had a *duty* to conform to reasonable standards of care and conduct that would ensure the plaintiff, Ms. Tompkins, against injury. Second, that duty had to be *breached* by the defendant airline. Third, that breach of duty must have *caused* the plaintiff's injuries. Finally, there had to be actual *harm* to the plaintiff.

The defendant's lawyer said that the airline breached no duty to Ms. Tompkins because the pilot avoided the crash. "Without the pilot's quick dive, the planes would have crashed, so how can the airline be at fault?" asked the defense lawyer.

Ms. Tompkins's lawyer strongly disagreed. "It was a clear day and visibility was at least 10 miles. Despite this, neither the pilot nor any crew member spotted the oncoming plane until it was five seconds away!" The lawyer's voice was firm, and she looked at each juror's face. "The pilot knew there were other planes in the area. He had flown that route many times before. He had a duty to maintain a lookout, but he did not do so. He failed in his duty and did not act properly under the conditions until the other plane was about five seconds away. Then the pilot made a steep dive without warning the passengers. In every way, he acted carelessly and negligently. He and the crew failed to keep a proper lookout and caused the situation that injured Ms. Tompkins."

LAW

## THE LAW IN ACTION

After hearing the testimony and arguments, the jury was given instructions by the judge. She explained that if jurors decided from the facts that the defendant had indeed been negligent, they ought to find for the plaintiff.

The jury deliberated for two hours and returned with its verdict. They agreed with Ms. Tompkins's lawyer that the airline was negligent because the pilot and crew failed to maintain a proper lookout.

### A Trial Involving Burglary

Later Jeff and Raul saw a criminal trial at the County Court Building. A man was charged with breaking and entering with intent to commit larceny. The defendant allegedly broke into a house late at night when the owner was away. A neighbor phoned the police when she heard glass breaking next door. When the police arrived, the accused was about to drive away from the house with a portable television, a stereo, and the homeowner's coin collection.

Before the trial, the prosecution and defense had worked hard to gather evidence and witnesses. The defendant had a choice of entering one of three pleas: guilty, not guilty, or no contest, which has the same legal effect as a guilty plea. He had pleaded not guilty.

From the moment he was arrested by the police, the rules of criminal procedure began to operate. It works in ways unlike civil procedure. Jeff's counselor explained that criminal procedure protects the rights of the accused, from arrest through trial, and tells how the process by which guilt or innocence is determined must operate.

"The main goal of criminal procedure," Mr. Hernandez said, "is to guarantee the individual's rights while protecting the rights of society, and to ensure fairness and justice in the court process. Somebody's guilt or innocence must be established through an orderly, precise, and uniform system in which constitutional freedoms and liberties are respected."

54   LAW

# THE LAW IN ACTION

Jeff and Raul knew many of the constitutional rights guaranteed to accused persons. They knew that the reason for having a jury in the courtroom was found in the U.S. Constitution. They heard someone in the spectator's section say that the county provided the accused with a defense lawyer because he could not afford one. Jeff and Raul also knew that the right to *counsel*—to be represented by a lawyer—was found in the Constitution.

It was fascinating to watch the defense lawyer cross-examine a witness for the prosecution. The witness was asked to identify the man she saw at the back door of the house the night of the burglary.

"Him. It was him." The witness pointed to the accused.

"How late at night was it when you say you saw the defendant at the back door of your neighbor's house?" the defense attorney asked.

"About 2 A.M.," answered the witness.

"It's usually rather dark at 2 A.M., isn't it?" the defense attorney asked.

"Well . . . uh . . . yes."

"There were no lights on anywhere in the vicinity of your house or your neighbor's, isn't that correct?"

"Yes."

"But you have testified that a man with blond hair and blue pants was at the back door of your neighbor's house at 2 A.M. on the night of the burglary. How can you be sure?"

"I'm really sure, I guess," the witness said.

"You were able to clearly tell and swear under oath that you could see the man's blond hair and blue pants."

"Well, I . . . I was sure. . . . I am sure!"

"And you were also quite sure," said the defense lawyer, "that the 'burglar,' as you called him, was about 5 foot 7. Are you still sure that the burglar was 5 foot 7?

"Well, it was dark . . . but, uh, yes. Yes, he was."

"I will now ask the defendant to stand," the lawyer said.

Jeff and Raul were surprised when the blond defendant rose from his chair. He was as tall as a basketball player. The people in the courtroom gasped.

LAW 55

## The Law in Action

"The defendant is almost 6 foot 5. You firmly claimed that the burglar was much shorter. Are you still sure this is the same person you saw outside your neighbor's back door?" asked the lawyer.

"No . . . no," the witness mumbled.

Despite this testimony, the accused was found guilty. The arresting police officer positively identified him, and his fingerprints were on the door and stolen items. He was sentenced to two years in the state penitentiary.

"Did you notice a court reporter toward the front of the courtroom tapping keys on a machine?" Mr. Hernandez asked Raul and Jeff.

"Yes, yes we did. Why is there a court reporter?" asked Jeff.

"The court reporter takes down every word said during the trial so that if any of the defendant's rights are denied or even partly withheld, and the defendant loses the trial, the record can be used as a basis for appeal. Often a criminal case can be reversed or returned to the court for a new trial if a right is denied. If a judge acts unfairly or with prejudice, the record will help to prove it, and it will help get a new trial for the defendant," Mr. Hernandez explained.

"And now that you have seen real trials," Mr. Hernandez continued, "you'll be able to get more out of the mock trial in which you will take part."

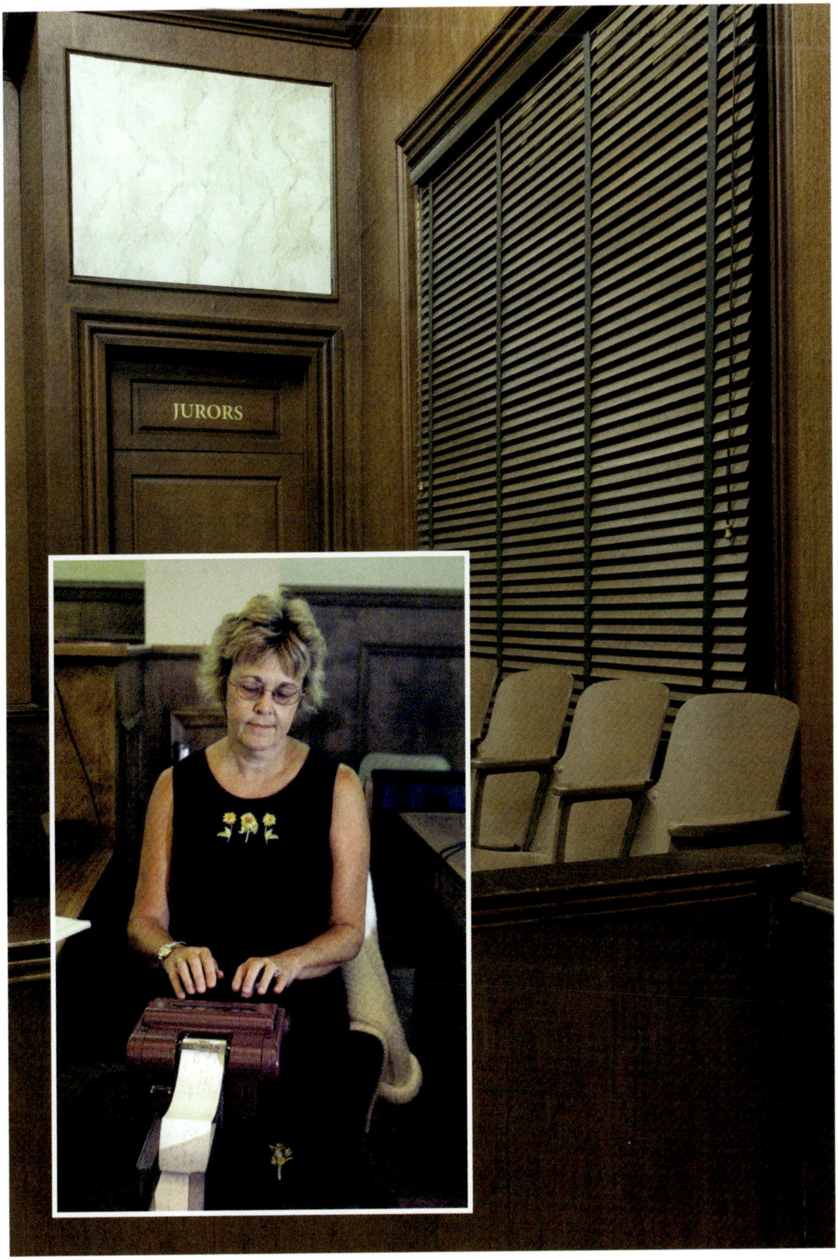
JURORS

East Franklin Street
To Estes Drive
South Columbia Street
Pizza Pub
Bagel Heaven
Nita Morning Globe
Parking
West Franklin Street
Sidewalk
Cut-Rate Liquor Outlet
Nita Municipal Lot
Sidewalk
Dorothy's Bar & Grill
Church Street
Rubino & Son
Parking Lot
Jewelers

# Planning a Mock Trial

Jeff decided to plan and conduct a mock trial with members of his troop. He asked Mr. Hernandez to be the judge. The counselor agreed. After discussing with other Scouts what kind of trial to hold, Jeff decided that a civil tort case would be fun to do.

Mr. Hernandez explained that this type of case was common. The most common tort cases involve an injured person seeking damages, for example, after an auto accident or slipping and falling. "The issue," he said, "is whether the injury was caused by someone's negligence, and, if so, what monetary damages would be sufficient to compensate the victim."

"How do we put on a case?" Jeff asked.

"Well," said Mr. Hernandez, "you could adapt the case that you and I witnessed, or just make up your own situation. For example, you could imagine how a car collision happened. Let's say a driver in one car is rushing to make a light and turns at the intersection, only to collide with a truck that may have run the red light. The car's driver is injured and has medical expenses. The car is pretty well totaled.

"If the driver sues the truck driver, the truck driver must be proven negligent. Could witnesses testify that the truck went into the intersection before the light changed? What if witnesses disagree with this point? What other factors might have caused the accident? Can witnesses testify to how fast the car was going? Do all the witnesses agree on this point? How fast should the car have been going given the weather conditions and time of day?

"You can make the case as simple or as complicated as you want. You can have one witness for each side (the two drivers), two witnesses, or more. You can even have an expert police witness testify to what the skid marks prove.

## Planning a Mock Trial

"Or maybe," Mr. Hernandez added, "you want to take a fact situation from one of the hundreds of mock trials that have already been done. The back of your *Law* merit badge pamphlet lists sources for mock trials."

Jeff made a list of the roles that had to be filled for the mock trial, in addition to the role of judge.

> **Roles for mock trial:**
>
> - Plaintiff
> - Defendant
> - Plaintiff's lawyer
> - Defendant's lawyer
> - Court clerk
> - Court reporter
> - Bailiff
> - Plaintiff's witnesses
> - Defendant's witnesses
> - Jurors

"Each role is important," Mr. Hernandez said. "The lawyers for both sides must present their cases clearly and try to persuade the jury. The witnesses must stick to the facts, and the jury must pay close attention to everything that is said. Each juror must make up his or her own mind about the evidence presented."

"What do the others do?" one Scout asked.

The counselor explained that the court clerk sets up the courtroom and keeps track of the court's records of the trial. "The court reporter makes notes of the important things said by the lawyers, witnesses, and judge. In a real trial, a word-for-word record is made. In this mock trial, you can write down important highlights. If you want to, you can tape-record the whole trial."

"That's a good idea," said Jeff. "Then we'll be able to review exactly what happened during the trial."

"You have chosen to do a mock civil trial with a jury," Mr. Hernandez said. "The trial follows a certain order and rules of procedure. After the jury is sworn in, the clerk will announce the name of the case and the name of the judge. Then, the plaintiff's lawyer will make an opening statement to lay out the charges and provide a summary of important facts. After that, the defendant's lawyer will make an opening statement. The lawyer will state the facts from the defendant's point of view and show facts that might weaken the plaintiff's case."

"Then the plaintiff's side will present its witnesses. All the witnesses will be sworn in by the clerk," said a Scout.

"That's correct," said the counselor. "After the plaintiff's side presents its witnesses and evidence, the defense will do the same. During cross-examination of each witness, the lawyers will try to explain, modify, or challenge what was said and presented by the opposing side.

"After witnesses have testified and cross-examination and rebuttal have ended, the defendant's lawyer makes a final argument. This is followed by the plaintiff's closing argument. Both sides present a summary of facts and make points in their favor in a way that clearly wraps up all the parts. They must present a sharp picture to the jury and leave a good impression with the jurors," the counselor explained.

"When the plaintiff completes the closing argument, the judge will give instructions to the jury that include the principles of law concerning the case and how those principles can be applied to the facts. The judge will then send the jury out of the courtroom to deliberate in secret. The jury will return its verdict and the judge will make a formal, official entry of the *judgment*. That will end the mock trial."

If your troop decided to hold a nonjury trial, the order of the trial would be similar to the jury trial except that jury selection, instructions to the jury, and fact-finding by the jury would not occur. In a nonjury case, the judge rules on both law and fact.

The key to a successful mock trial is careful preparation. Every trial lawyer knows that success depends on being well prepared to present the best possible case and to foresee what the other side might do. For the mock trial, you should also prepare for your role with care. When the trial is over, talk about how you felt in the role you played. Ask the others for their opinions.

> When you are sworn in as a witness, you make a formal pledge or promise to tell the truth. You take an oath saying that what you are about to say is the truth.

## Lawyers Outside of Court

In his talks with Mr. Hernandez, Jeff learned that many lawyers seldom go into court. His counselor arranged for him to meet a few of them to talk about what they do.

Because law is deeply involved in every aspect of life, businesses, banks, government, real estate companies, and many other concerns must employ men and women who understand law. Lawyers also work in state and federal legislatures, city and town councils, and other areas of government.

## Planning a Mock Trial

Chances are good that at least one of the officers at your local bank is a lawyer or has had some legal training. Title companies that record and insure property transactions, such as land and house sales, employ lawyers to make sure transactions go smoothly and title transfers are proper in all respects.

Government departments, commissions, committees, bureaus, and offices employ lawyers to ensure proper operation. These lawyers rarely go to court. Instead, they keep aware of new laws, rules, and regulations that concern their departments.

"I'm a full-time lawyer for the store," Ms. Jackson told Jeff. "My only client is the store. Because this is one of the largest department stores in the country and is owned by a company that has other stores like this one all over the United States, the company employs a staff of lawyers."

Jeff was visiting Ms. Jackson's office on the top floor of a large department store where his family often shopped. Ms. Jackson was explaining what a *corporation counsel*, a lawyer for a corporation, does.

"My responsibility is to keep the company out of court. Going to court involves time, trouble, and money. The company wants to avoid *litigation* or lawsuits. So what I do is research the laws, carefully read contracts, and advise the owners and managers of the company how to stay out of court," Ms. Jackson said.

"You must be busy," Jeff said.

"Believe me, we are! But there is more! The U.S. government makes rules and regulations concerning prices we can charge our customers, wages we must pay store employees, and many other things. The legal department must keep up with those laws and guidelines, too. We also work closely with the company accountants concerning taxes."

Jeff rose to leave and extended his hand to shake Ms. Jackson's. "Thank you for taking the time to talk to me about your duties and responsibilities," Jeff said.

As Jeff left the store, he saw a familiar face. It was Mr. Robertson, another counselor for the Law merit badge who was a good friend of Mr. Hernandez.

"Hello, Jeff," called Mr. Robertson. "What are you doing downtown?"

"I'm working on my Law merit badge and just spoke to Ms. Jackson about what lawyers who work for stores do." Jeff then had a great idea. Mr. Robertson is the *city attorney*—a lawyer who works for the local government. What a chance to find out what government lawyers do! "Do you happen to have a spare minute or two, Mr. Robertson?" Jeff asked.

"Certainly. I was just going to see Mr. Harrington, the lawyer at the bank, to talk about how to pay for the new swimming pool at the park. That's part of my responsibility. I'm going to check on the loan agreement with the bank," explained Mr. Robertson.

Jeff told Mr. Robertson about requirement 7. Mr. Robertson was happy to tell Jeff about some of the things the city attorney does.

Mr. Robertson explained that laws passed by the city council are called *ordinances* and that he writes such laws in proper legal form. He also represents the city in court when necessary, and he carefully reads and helps prepare contracts for city purchases and services.

"The city prosecutor works for me," Mr. Robertson said. "When the police arrest a suspect who may have violated a city ordinance, the *city prosecutor* represents the city in court. He or she also gives advice to the police department in many areas. While the prosecutor handles prosecutions and police-related matters, I work on civil law matters. Because my responsibility is to try to keep the city out of court, the prosecutor is in court a lot more than I am."

"How do you keep the city out of court?" Jeff asked.

---

Law Day, which falls on May 1 each year, is a major national celebration of the rule of law and our heritage of liberty under law. Each year, the American Bar Association conducts a special program to help celebrate the day. You will find plenty of information about law and Law Day by visiting the ABA's website. See the resources section for more information.

LAW   63

## Finding a Lawyer

Mr. Hernandez gave Jeff an imaginary problem to consider. "Let's suppose that Mr. Jenkins bought and paid for a refrigerator at a store. The salesperson said the refrigerator was new, but when it arrived, it was used and didn't work properly. Mr. Jenkins asked the store to take it back and refund his money or replace it with a new refrigerator. The store refused to do anything, and Mr. Jenkins seems to be left with a useless refrigerator.

"Now Jeff, I'm not asking you to solve the legal issues here," Mr. Hernandez said. "Just explain what you think Mr. Jenkins should do. Remember that he doesn't have enough money to pay for a lawyer."

In his research, Jeff learned a lot about how to find a lawyer and legal assistance. Mr. Jenkins should contact a consumer protection agency or go to small claims court if the value of the refrigerator is within a certain amount. Another thing he could do is call a legal assistance service. If he cannot find one, he should get in touch with the bar association.

Any local or state bar association can refer you to a legal aid service. Legal aid services offer the help of a lawyer for free, or, at most, for a small fee to people who can't afford a lawyer. Also, some charitable organizations help people obtain legal services when they cannot afford to pay.

One helpful agency is the Legal Services Corporation, a private, nonprofit corporation established by Congress in 1974 to ensure equal access to justice under the law for all Americans. It offers legal aid in every state. Bar associations and government public defender offices also offer free legal advice and assistance.

# Planning a Mock Trial

> Most legal assistance groups do not usually become involved in criminal cases. In criminal cases, a judge will appoint a public defender if the accused person cannot afford a lawyer. Public defenders handle the defense of criminally accused people, and legal aid is available for those who cannot afford to pay. Jeff found out that lawyers have a professional responsibility to make the legal system work for everybody—not just those who can pay.
>
> People who *can* afford to pay for legal services can still contact the local or state bar association and ask for the Lawyer Referral Service. The service can help find a lawyer who can assist them in the particular area of law in which they need help. The service also can make an appointment with a lawyer for a certain fee.
>
> Jeff discovered that the internet is a great way to find lawyers, too. The American Bar Association has a website at www.findlegalhelp.org that can help people find a lawyer referral service near them. The ABA offers a number of public services and can be found on the web at www.americanbar.org.

"Well, as I said, by carefully reading contracts and giving advice to the mayor, the city council, and the city manager on how to avoid legal problems. I also make sure city ordinances are fair and within the limits set by the state and federal governments. You see, some areas are handled solely by the federal and state governments. I have to make sure the city's ordinances do not exceed their authority," Mr. Robertson said.

As Mr. Robertson left, Jeff decided to meet with his counselor and report on what he learned.

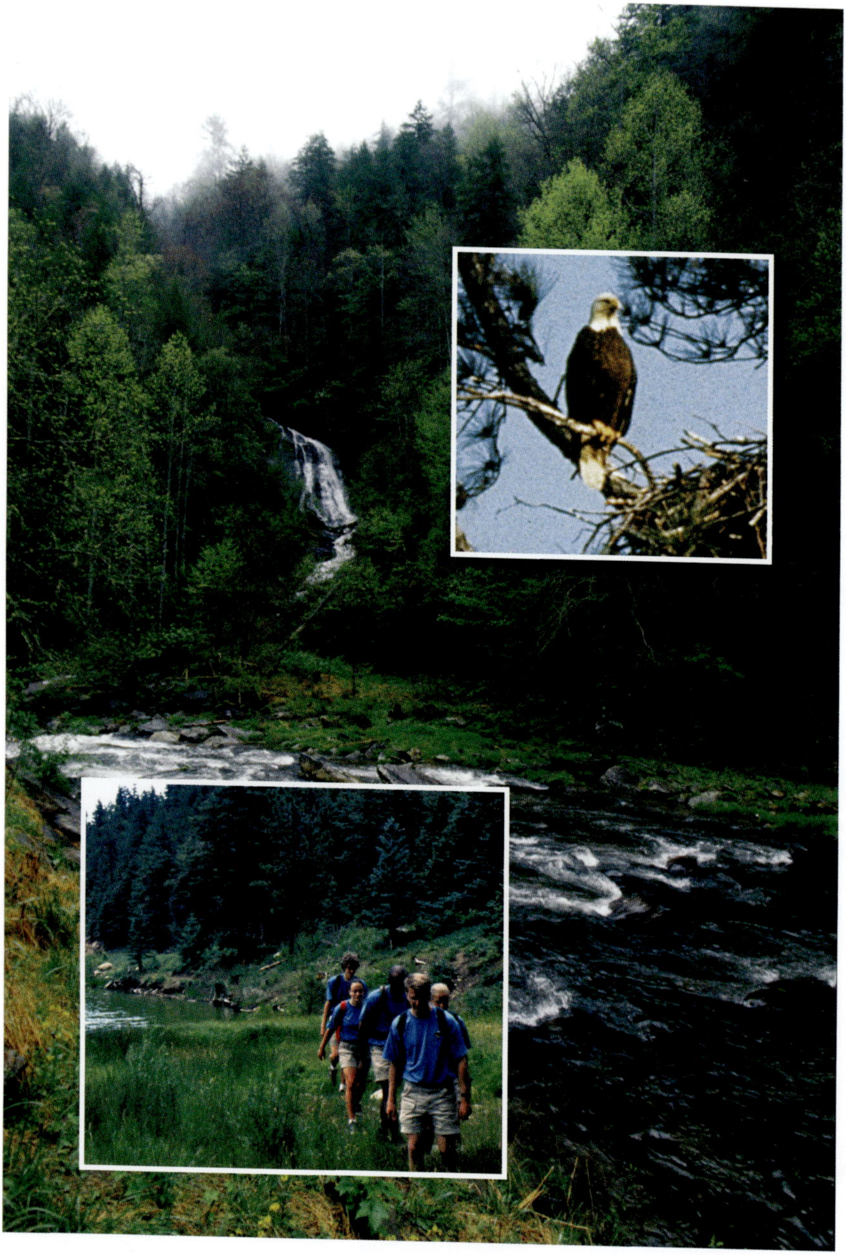

# Emerging Law

At Mr. Hernandez's suggestion, Jeff turned his attention to learning about emerging law. Jeff had been studying the environment in his science class at school and was particularly interested in finding out about environmental law. He found the Environmental Protection Agency's website to be very useful.

## Environmental Law

Jeff read that the modern environmental movement began with the passage of the **National Environmental Policy Act of 1969.** This is the basic national charter for environmental protection that establishes policy, sets goals, and provides means for carrying out the policy.

More than a dozen major statutes, or laws, form the legal basis for the programs of the Environmental Protection Agency. One important law under this umbrella is the **Clear Air Act,** passed in 1970, which regulates air emissions to protect public health and the environment. In 1977, this act was amended to address problems such as acid rain, ground-level ozone, and air toxics.

The **Clean Water Act** came along in 1977 amidst growing public awareness and concern for controlling water pollution. This act gives the EPA the authority to regulate the discharge of pollutants into America's waterways, rivers, lakes, and streams. It is now against the law for any person to discharge any pollutant into navigable waters without a permit.

Jeff also read about the **Endangered Species Act,** which became law in 1973. The U.S. Fish and Wildlife Service under the Department of the Interior maintains the list of 1,077 endangered species (644 are plants) and 317 threatened species (150 are plants).

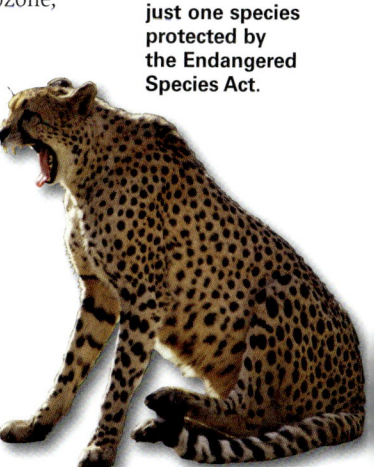

The cheetah is just one species protected by the Endangered Species Act.

# Emerging Law

This act established a program for the conservation of threatened and endangered plants and animals and the habitats where they are found. Fish, birds, reptiles, mammals, crustaceans, flowers, grasses, and trees can be found on this list. Jeff was pleased to know anyone can petition the Fish and Wildlife Service to include a species on the list.

Amendments to the law allow the EPA to ban certain pesticides or restrict their use if an endangered species will be negatively affected.

Jeff noticed that the EPA's role expanded further in 1990, when the **Pollution Prevention Act** focused industry, government, and public attention on reducing pollution through cost-effective changes in production, operation, and use of raw materials.

In other words, industries are now being challenged to increase efficiency in their use of energy, water, and other natural resources. They must protect our resources through conservation.

Jeff learned that other acts passed in recent years cover corporate responsibility for polluting the environment knowingly or through a tragic mishap, such as a chemical leak.

## Copyright, Computers, and the Internet

Now that he had learned so much about emerging environmental law, Jeff decided that for his next project he would look up information on copyright, computers, and the internet. In a telephone conversation, Mr. Hernandez told Jeff that copyright is so important it is covered in the U.S. Constitution.

"The Constitution states that Congress shall have the power to promote the progress of science and useful arts by securing for limited times to authors and inventors the exclusive right to their respective writings and discoveries," Mr. Hernandez told Jeff. "Did you know whenever you write a story or create a drawing, you automatically own the copyright?"

"No, I didn't know that. You mean, even for a project at school?" Jeff asked.

"Yes, even for a project at school! Copyright is a form of protection given to authors or creators of 'original works of authorship' including literary, dramatic, musical, artistic, and other intellectual works. What that basically means is, as the author of the work, you alone have the rights to make and distribute copies of it, perform your work publicly, or make *derivative works,* such as modifications, adaptations, or translations of the work into another medium. It is illegal for anyone to do any of these things without your permission."

Mr. Hernandez added that there were some exceptions and limitations to a person's rights as a copyright holder. "One major limitation," he said, "is the doctrine of fair use."

"You see, Jeff, the *fair use doctrine* allows limited copying of copyrighted works for educational and research purposes. The copyright law allows reproduction for purposes of criticism, news reporting, teaching, scholarship, or research. This allows your teacher to hand out short excerpts from a book, or for a reporter to quote from a particular work of art, writing, or speech. If an author claims that his or her work has been used without permission, courts must weigh the evidence to determine whether a particular use of a copyrighted work is permitted under fair use, or if it is, instead, an infringement of copyright."

"What about the internet? Is information on websites protected by copyright law?"

"You bet," said Mr. Hernandez. "Most webpages, including the information on them and the computer code used to create them, are protected by copyright law."

"How is copyright protected if the internet is a worldwide network?" Jeff asked.

"Good question, Jeff," Mr. Hernandez said approvingly. "Because the internet is a global resource, copyrighted work on the web is governed by an international treaty, called the **Berne Convention for the Protection of Literary and Artistic Works.** The convention, however, allows individual countries to determine what is and isn't protected."

"What about computer software programs?" Jeff asked.

"Most software, including free software, is protected by copyright; it is not in the public domain. This means it is protected by law. All software is copyrighted on creation. No piece of software has been in existence long enough to pass into public domain. The only software currently available in the public domain is there because the owner has expressly allowed it to be. This kind of software is clearly labeled."

## Yours, Mine, and Ours

**Public domain** is described as a body of work—books, songs, music, and software are examples—that is not protected by copyright law and that, in effect, belongs to the public at large, to be used freely by the public. It could be that the copyright has expired, or that the creation consists solely of facts or ideas, or is printed by the Government Printing Office.

"How long does copyright protection last?" Jeff asked.

"Copyrights do not last forever but they do last a long time. Under current laws, copyright protection starts from the moment of creation of the work and continues until 70 years after the death of the author or artist."

"What does public domain mean exactly?" Jeff asked.

"When a copyright expires, the work falls into the *public domain,* meaning anyone can use it," explained Mr. Hernandez. "That's why you can copy artists like Leonardo da Vinci and writers like Shakespeare all you want. Because of changes to the law in the 1970s, you cannot assume any work is in the public domain unless it was first published before 1923."

Mr. Hernandez said another thing to keep in mind when looking at copyrighted works posted on the web is that just because you are reading it there doesn't mean it is there legally. "A good rule of thumb," he said, "is to always get permission to use a copyrighted online work from the owner of that work, not from a secondary source like the webmaster."

Some authors and artists choose to make it clear that other people can use their work. They may have a Creative Commons license or other wording that gives people permission to use or copy their work as if it were in the public domain. Creative Commons makes available art, music, and other works that give permission for you to copy. See the resources section for more information.

## Immigration Law

We are a nation founded by immigrants. Yet disputes about who is permitted to visit or live in the United States and what type of immigration process should be put in place have existed since its foundation. Immigration law determines who is permitted to visit or live in the U.S. and what process they should follow to do so. The goal of our immigration laws and the courts that enforce these laws is, in part, to bring order and fairness to our immigration system.

## Patent Law

The patent laws in the United States are among the oldest of our country's laws, dating to 1790. Patent law protects the inventor of a new product who has obtained a patent on that product. Generally, patent owners can prevent others from making, using, selling, or importing the patented invention for 20 years. If someone uses an invention without the inventor's permission, the inventor can sue for patent infringement.

The U.S. Patent and Trademark Office examines patent applications that are filed by inventors. Patent examiners must decide if the inventor's claimed invention is sufficiently different from technology that is already available to the public, sufficiently described in the patent application so that it can be readily put to some practical use by a skilled engineer reading the patent, sufficiently definite so that it is reasonably clear what technology the patent will and will not cover, and sufficiently concrete. Mere ideas and concepts, for example, cannot be patented because they are not sufficiently concrete. Once the patent examiner is satisfied that a patent can be granted, the examiner will identify the specific claims that were found to be patentable and permit a patent to be issued to the inventor.

## Biotechnology Law

Biotechnology is the use of living systems and organisms to develop or make useful products, such as in forest products, petroleum, agriculture, and medicine. Like some other high-tech industries, it relies heavily on intellectual property for its value, so patent filing is critical.

Biotechnology is a highly regulated industry, requiring filing with federal organizations. Companies making pharmaceutical products, for example, must file with the U.S. Food and Drug

Administration and the European Union's European Medicines Agency. This requires the companies to perform structured trials of the product to measure safety and effectiveness. The time from concept to market for most biotech products is very long and the cost is high, in part because of the multiyear (in many cases) regulatory process and in part because of the sheer technical complexity of developing these products. It is common for a biotech medical product to take more than 12 years to progress from concept to market.

Biotechnology can also involve securities law, which is important when seeking funding, and international law, in order to market the product worldwide.

## Privacy Law

Privacy has become a crucial concern in recent decades, although some privacy laws date to the Bill of Rights. Privacy is a broad concept that encompasses the rights of an individual to be free from intrusion and interference from governments, businesses, and other people.

Laws pertaining to freedom from government intrusion include the Fourth Amendment to the U.S. Constitution, which protects people from unreasonable searches and seizures of their homes, cars, documents, computers, and mobile devices. Additionally, the federal **Privacy Act of 1974** requires federal agencies to safeguard their records containing people's personal information, such as educational, financial, medical, criminal, or employment records. Agencies may not disclose this kind of personal information without authorization.

Various laws impose privacy requirements on businesses to notify consumers of what kinds of information they gather, how they use the information, the conditions under which they share or disclose information, how they safeguard information from unauthorized disclosure or use, and how they manage and update information. These are the typical topics covered by the privacy policies of businesses and their websites.

Privacy law also allows people to bring lawsuits against others for violating their privacy in various ways. Such laws prohibit unreasonable intrusion into private areas, such as a photographer standing right outside someone's house taking pictures of events inside through an open window. Other laws focus on false light, which is publishing a highly offensive and misleading story or information that distorts a person's image. Imagine that a newspaper published a picture of an ordinary citizen who coincidentally happened to walk out of a building next to a notorious criminal. The picture of them together might suggest that the citizen is a friend or business partner of the criminal.

## International Law

International law is a set of rules and regulations by which countries, organizations, and people throughout the world interact with each other and with citizens of different countries. There are two general categories of international law: public and private. Public international law deals with relationships between nations or between a nation and organizations or people from other countries. Private international law deals with disputes between citizens of different countries or businesses from different countries, especially when there is a question of which country's laws apply or where the dispute should be resolved. Certain courts and bodies such as the United Nations Security Council have the power to decide cases of international law.

The Do-Not-Call Registry Act allows consumers to register their phone numbers in order to limit calls from telemarketers.

# Careers in the Legal Profession

Jeff reported his findings to Mr. Hernandez on the two areas of emerging law he had selected for requirement 11.

"You're almost finished with your Law merit badge requirements," Mr. Hernandez said. "All you need to do now is study the requirements for becoming a lawyer, find out how judges are selected in this state, and list 15 occupations that deal with law or legal processes. Think you can do that?"

"Sure," said Jeff. After talking to Mr. Hernandez and other lawyers, Jeff knew it took a lot of training to become a lawyer. First you have to go to college and then on to law school.

## Becoming a Lawyer

Mr. Hernandez had told Jeff that good lawyers should be naturally inquisitive, able to think logically, and able to recognize the core issues of a problem. Because lawyers have to deal with many different people, Jeff thought that patience, integrity, determination, and a sense of humanity also were important qualities for a lawyer to possess.

Jeff discovered that no special course of study is required in college to prepare for law school. Many law students have backgrounds in government, political science, sociology, and psychology. Many business, accounting, and economics majors go on to law school. Because law is related to nearly every human activity, Jeff thought that the best background would include a well-rounded, general knowledge of many subjects.

More than 125,000 law students in the United States are in full-time courses of study, which take three years to complete. A few thousand are in part-time or evening law school programs, which usually take four years. Summertime positions working for law firms, judges, courts, or in other law-related areas provide firsthand knowledge of how the law operates.

> To be admitted to a law school, a person should have good grades in college and a good score on the Law School Admissions Test (LSAT).

= CAREERS IN THE LEGAL PROFESSION

In law school, *moot court,* or mock trial, competition helps sharpen students' courtroom skills. Many schools have legal aid clinics and other programs in which students assist citizens with actual legal problems.

## Becoming a Judge

Justice Felix Frankfurter once said that judges should be a combination of "the historian, the philosopher, and the prophet" and have "something of the creative artist in them." Justice Frankfurter's description makes sense, but how are the right people chosen for this powerful, responsible role?

In more than half the states, trial court judges are selected by elections—nonpartisan in 22 states, partisan in 12. In partisan election states, Jeff noted, judges run in elections and are identified by political party label. In nonpartisan elections, judges are not identified by party affiliation.

## State Bar Examinations

In general, nobody becomes a lawyer simply by graduating from law school. Another step must be taken. Almost every law school graduate who wishes to become a practicing lawyer must pass a state bar examination. The bar examination is a written test administered by the state's bar admission agency, which is often titled the Board of Bar Examiners. The exam is given over a period of several days and demands preparation, concentration, and skill. It asks questions about issues and subjects the applicant might face as a lawyer. It tests knowledge of many legal areas, including trusts, wills, estates, and civil and criminal law. The bar admission agency might also require an oral examination.

The highest court of each state usually has jurisdiction over the bar admission process for that state. But in some states, the responsibility for investigating candidates is given to state and local bar associations.

## Your State's Requirements

To find out the requirements for becoming a lawyer in your state, write to the state bar admission agency, which is usually located in your state capital. Or contact the National Conference of Bar Examiners. See the resources section in this pamphlet.

The candidate for the judgeship campaigns exactly like another other candidate for political office. Jeff wondered whether this was a good way to make sure the best people become judges. He thought that some people might be elected as judges just because they are active in politics and speak well, while some good lawyers might be overlooked because they were not seeking to get the attention of a political party. Jeff also considered that elected judges might be partial to the causes of their own political party.

In a few states, he discovered, all or some of the judges are appointed to office by the governor with the consent and confirmation of a legislative body or the state legislature.

This approach, called the Missouri Plan, works this way. The state legislature chooses a panel of impartial and well-respected lawyers and nonlawyers. An equal number is chosen from each major political party. The panel searches for the finest candidates for judicial office and submits their list, usually of three names, to the governor. The governor must appoint one of these people. The choices are not listed by political party and the governor should not know the party labels. After the governor chooses, the new judge serves for a period of time. After a certain term, usually six years, the judge's record goes before the people.

"How do the people make a choice?" Jeff asked Mr. Hernandez.

"The only question on the ballot for judges will say, 'Should Judge Smith be retained in office?' No party identity is listed on the ballot. The judge does not have to run against other judges or candidates—only on his or her record. If the people say yes, the judge stays on the bench for another term."

"And what if the people say no?"

"Then the judge is no longer a judge and the governor again appoints a person from a list submitted by the panel," Mr. Hernandez explained.

Jeff wondered if the Missouri Plan was the best way to select judges. "They still have to sort of run for reelection. I'm just not sure that judges should have that much to do with elections and politics."

"There is probably no perfect way to choose judges, Jeff. People find positive and negative points with the election, appointment, and Missouri Plan methods. You can decide for yourself."

# Other Occupations in the Legal Profession

By now Jeff had talked to a lot of lawyers. And in visiting lawyers' offices, the courts, and the police, he had found plenty of other occupations in law. As he handed his list of law-connected careers to Mr. Hernandez, Jeff said, "There are lots of positions that have to do with law, aren't there?"

"Sure are," Mr. Hernandez agreed.

He began reading: "Uniformed police officer or sheriff's police officer, police detective, prison official, parole officer, juvenile officer, probation officer—Jeff, this list is really quite good."

"Thank you," Jeff smiled.

His counselor read more: "Court clerk, court bailiff—Say, do you know what the bailiff does?"

"The *bailiff* acts as the courtroom police," Jeff answered. "The bailiff helps keep the courtroom spectators, and sometimes the participants, orderly. The judge can sometimes have the bailiff serve subpoenas to witnesses, too."

"Judge, court reporter, legal secretary," Mr. Hernandez continued. "Legal secretaries help lawyers prepare papers and legal briefs for cases and write letters to clients and other parties. They perform other office duties and must understand the language of law."

Jeff also listed *paralegal*. The paralegal takes on some of the routine but important duties of a lawyer, such as researching, interviewing clients, and preparing papers. Jeff added FBI agent, state policeman, and private detective to his list. Private detectives must know the legal limits of their work. State police officers must know and enforce state laws while preserving the rights of citizens. FBI agents often prepare for their work by taking law and criminology courses.

Jeff also listed government officials who work for local, state, or federal governments. They must be aware of the law and how it affects their duties. "Elected legislators make laws, and nonelected officials fulfill responsibilities within the framework of those laws."

He also learned that business people, bankers, real estate personnel, and accountants must be aware of the law in their work. "When a real estate agent sells an interest in property, like a farm, a house, or an apartment building, the agent deals with property law," Jeff explained to his counselor.

"You are certainly right, Jeff," said Mr. Hernandez. "The law is everybody's business and concern."

---

The **court bailiff** helps keep order in the court.

The **paralegal** has some legal education but usually not as much as lawyers.

# Resources About Law

## Scouting Literature
*Citizenship in the Nation, Citizenship in the World,* and *Crime Prevention* merit badge pamphlets

> With your parent's permission, visit the Boy Scouts of America's official retail website, www.scoutshop.org, for a complete listing of all merit badge pamphlets and other helpful Scouting materials and supplies.

## Books

Aaseng, Nathan. *You Are the Juror.* Oliver Press, 1997.

Abadinsky, Howard. *Law, Courts, and Justice in America,* 7th ed. Waveland Press, Inc., 2014.

Abramson, Jeffrey. *We, the Jury: The Jury System and the Ideal of Democracy.* Harvard University Press, 2000.

Adler, Stephen J. *Jury: Trial and Error in the American Courtroom.* Crown Publishing, 1994.

American Bar Association Division for Public Education. *A Life in the Law.* American Bar Association, 2010.

Arbetman, Lee P., and Richard L. Roe. *Great Trials in American History: Civil War to the Present.* McGraw-Hill, 1985.

Besenjak, Cheryl. *Copyright Plain & Simple.* Career Press, 2000.

Bjornlund, Lydia D. *The U.S. Constitution: Blueprint for Democracy.* Lucent Books, 1999.

Bray, Ilona, J.D., *U.S. Immigration Made Easy,* 18th edition. Nolo, 2017.

Carrel, Annette. *It's the Law: A Young Person's Guide to Our Legal System.* Volcano Press, 1994.

Emert, Phyllis Raybin. *Top Lawyers and Their Famous Cases.* Oliver Press, 1996.

Greenhaven Press. *Civil Liberties: Opposing Viewpoints.* Greenhaven Press, 2013.

Irons, Peter. *The Courage of Their Convictions.* Free Press, 2015.

Knight, Alfred H. *The Life of the Law: The People and Cases That Have Shaped Our Society From King Alfred to Rodney King.* Oxford University Press, 1998.

Lee, Harper. *To Kill a Mockingbird.* Harper Perennial Modern Classics, 2002.

# Resources About Law

Lipson, Eric B., and Greta B. Lipson. *Everyday Law for Young Citizens.* Teaching and Learning Company, 2000.

McGraw-Hill Education. *Street Law: A Course in Practical Law,* student edition. McGraw-Hill Education, 2016.

Monk, Linda R. *The Bill of Rights: A User's Guide,* 4th ed. Close Up Foundation, 2004.

Morin, Isobel V. *Our Changing Constitution: How and Why We Have Amended It.* Millbrook Press, 1998.

National Crime Prevention Council Staff. *Community Works: Smart Teens Make Safer Communities.* National Crime Prevention Council, 1999.

Phelan, Margaret and James Gillespie, *Immigration Law Handbook,* 10th edition. Oxford University Press, 2018.

Renstrom, Peter G. *The American Law Dictionary.* A B C–CLIO, 1991.

## Organizations and Websites

**American Bar Association Division for Public Education**
321 N. Clark St.
Chicago, IL 60654
Website: www.americanbar.org/groups/public_education.html

**Creative Commons**
Website: https://creativecommons.org

**Environmental Protection Agency**
1200 Pennsylvania Ave., NW
Washington, DC 20460
Website: www.epa.gov/lawsregs/index.html

**National Association of Youth Courts**
2700 University Blvd., #402
Tuscaloosa, AL 35401
Website: www.youthcourt.net

**National Conference of Bar Examiners**
302 S. Bedford St.
Madison, WI 53703-3622
Website: www.ncbex.org

**Social Studies School Service**
P.O. Box 802
Culver City, CA 90232
Toll-free telephone: 800-421-4246
Website: www.socialstudies.com

**Street Law**
1010 Wayne Ave., Suite 870
Silver Spring, MD 20910
Telephone: 301-589-1130
Website: www.streetlaw.org

Bar associations everywhere support public legal education. To get an idea of the range of activities and the resources available, visit the following websites. The **New York State Bar Association** has a Law, Youth, and Citizenship program that offers mock trial tournaments, summer courses, and programs that promote citizenship and law-related education. Visit its website at www.nysba.org. The **Pennsylvania Bar Association,** at www.pabar.org, provides information for all kinds of youth-related programs and activities. The **State Bar of Texas** can be found on the web at www.texasbar.com. Its Law-Related Education, an arm of the association, sponsors an editorial contest and offers teacher in-service programs. The **Washington State Bar Association,** at www.wsba.org, offers a huge range of activities.

## Acknowledgments

The Boy Scouts of America would like to acknowledge Charles White of the American Bar Association for his expertise in developing and revising the *Law* merit badge pamphlet, and Judge Aymer L. "Buck" Curtin of the Alachua County Court in Gainesville, Florida, for his suggestions and advice on emerging law.

Thanks also to the American Bar Association; Special Committee on Youth Education for Citizenship; Joel F. Henning and Norman Gross (original editors); and Michael Froman (author of the 1975 edition) for their role with the *Law* merit badge pamphlet.

Thanks to the Law Library at Texas Wesleyan School of Law in Fort Worth for allowing the use of facilities there for a photo shoot. We are grateful to Robert E. Corlew III, chancellor of the 16th Judicial District, State of Tennessee, for facilitating a ph... courthouse ...

The B... would like ... Departmen... communit... a photo sh... badge pan...

The ... grateful to ... serving on ... Subcomm... made in u...

## Photo and Illustration Credits

Federal Bureau of Investigation, courtesy—page 42

Federal Trade Commission, courtesy—page 47

National Park Service, Frederick Douglass National Historic Site, courtesy—page 17

Shutterstock.com—cover *(badge,* ©Natan86; *gavel,* ©Cesar M. Romero; *handcuffs,* ©Veronica Louro; *quill pen,* ©Davydenko Yuliia; *U.S. Capitol,* ©Songquan Deng); pages 8 (©Ivelin Radkov), 11 (©David Smart), 13 *(gavel,* ©Billion Photos; *traffic officer,* ©bikeriderlondon; *students,* ©Monkey Business Images; *parking sign,* ©Icatnews; *background,* ©Reinhold Leitner), 18 (©bikeriderlondon), 20 (©larry1235), 26 (©everything possible), 36 *(police and flags,* ©Dale A Stork), 39 (©bikerider-... media), ...st), 55 ...rtroom, ...kground, ...23 ...s not ...ty ...couts ...strations) ...urt